Anthracite People
Families, Unions and Work, 1900-1940

JOHN BODNAR

Commonwealth of Pennsylvania
PENNSYLVANIA HISTORICAL
AND MUSEUM COMMISSION
Harrisburg, 1983

SUPPORTED BY A GRANT FROM:

**PENNSYLVANIA
HUMANITIES
COUNCIL**

A STATEWIDE FUNDING ORGANIZATION FUNDED IN PART BY THE NATIONAL ENDOWMENT FOR THE HUMANITIES

Opinions and ideas expressed in this book do not necessarily represent the views of the Pennsylvania Humanities Council or those of the National Endowment for the Humanities.

Acknowledgments

RECONSTRUCTING the history of the mining families of the Nanticoke area and the Wyoming Valley required assistance from many sources. Residents of the region not only graciously allowed me into their homes but generously shared their recollections and photographs and even put me in touch with friends who provided additional information. Jule Znaniecki was absolutely essential in helping locate respondents in Nanticoke, and Joseph Molski opened my way into the Glen Lyon and Wanamie areas. Anthony Piscotty also provided valuable leads, particularly when he put me in touch with Chester Brozena. Joseph Sudol and John Sarnowski patiently submitted to several interviewing sessions and Mr. Sudol and Leonard Wydotis generously opened up their homes for group meetings.

The Wyoming Historical and Geological Society was an indispensible aid and its then director, William Seiner, assisted me throughout the project with valuable leads and photographs. I thank him and his staff. The Pennsylvania Historical and Museum Commission, Larry E. Tise, Executive Director, approved the project. The work was carried out under Harry E. Wipkey, Director of the Bureau of Archives and History. Harold L. Myers, Associate Historian, looked after its publication. Matthew S. Magda, Associate Historian, displayed characteristic persistence in getting me to finish this manuscript and in completing many project details. I must also acknowledge the assistance of the Oral History Research Center of Indiana University in some of the transcribing. The project benefitted throughout from the expert typing of Joanne Bornman and Pat McKee and the proofreading of Roxane Kauffman. Generous financial assistance was provided by the Pennsylvania Humanities Council. I would also like to thank my wife, Donna, for the hours of typing and for the support she has given me.

Finally, it bears mentioning that all the interviews used in this book were conducted in 1981 by the author. The only exceptions are the Wierzorek interview, in 1977, and the Skrovanski interview, in 1978, both very capably done by Angela Staskavage; the Hosey interview, conducted in 1977 by James Rodechko; and the Niziolek interview, conducted in 1977 by Kenneth Hughes.

JOHN BODNAR
Indiana University, Bloomington

Introduction

ON Good Friday morning in April, 1936, Thomas Maloney went downstairs in his Wilkes-Barre home to dress his five-year-old son. His wife, who was feeling ill, remained upstairs in bed. Maloney noticed a package in the day's mail wrapped in plain brown paper and marked "sample." As he opened the package it exploded, killing him and his young boy. That day bombs were also received by a former sheriff and by a Luzerne County judge. The calm of an Easter weekend was shattered by a sudden thrust of violence, the kind that had become all too familiar in the northern anthracite coal fields of eastern Pennsylvania.

The killing of Thomas Maloney was the culmination of the violence and protest which, in the early 1930's, had shaken to its foundation the social order of the Wyoming Valley from Wilkes-Barre to Nanticoke. Maloney had been the leader of a band of insurgents, called the United Anthracite Miners of Pennsylvania (UAM), which had fought bitterly against the entrenched power of its old union, the United Mine Workers of America (UMW), and the local coal companies, such as Glen Alden. Maloney and officials of the UAM had been arrested and tried for disregarding a strike injunction in 1935, a sensational case which not only brought thousands of miners to Wilkes-Barre to rally in the defendants' behalf but resulted also in the bombing of the car of the presiding judge.

It may seem extraordinary for hard-coal miners to challenge the union to which they were so closely tied by tradition, but by the third decade of the twentieth century the anthracite industry of eastern Pennsylvania was in trouble, and with it its union. The peak of hard-coal production had been reached in 1917 and would never be reached again. Traditional consumers had begun the switch to oil and gas, and prospects were dim. Although the shifting of markets and the decline of an industry are not unknown to American business, the impact of industrial shutdown and economic dislocation on the people of a community or region is seldom understood.

In every instance where an industry flourishes, people construct a social system of family groupings and communities, incorporating values and behavior patterns shaped by that industry's economy and dependent upon its good health and continued existence. The people of the anthracite region conformed to this pattern. Emigrating from the rural areas and villages of Europe, beginning in the latter decades of the nineteenth century, the emigrants forged a society which was structured not only to take advantage of the work opportunities offered by anthracite mining,

1

but also to deal with economic difficulties from which that industry suffered. Fundamental to their society was a strong network of kinship and communal relationships which sustained its members through such means as the labor of children, assistance from family in the procurement of work, communal social activities, and emotional support during periods of mourning.

But family and community provided insufficient means for these hard-pressed people to achieve all that was necessary to make ends meet. Consequently, they applied their communal approach to the problem of economic security by supporting the United Mine Workers of America. With a rich legacy of union support from the nineteenth century and from the great Anthracite Strike of 1902, they were consistent in their support of a vigorous union to achieve better wages and working conditions.

By 1932, however, economic difficulties were mounting and these people faced increasing pressure. Their union was failing to address their real concerns and was perceived to be somewhat corrupt by the rank and file. For them in fact, the union had made itself an ally of the coal companies, who for decades had controlled so much of their lives, their jobs, their local politics, and their tax assessments. In fact, anthracite people held these companies singularly responsible for preventing other types of industry from locating in the hard-coal regions and competing with them for their "captive" labor.

In this little book the recollections of anthracite people are presented. Their memoirs are focused particularly on the three decades that began in 1920, during which time, as their economic base deteriorated, they fought crucial battles and made vital decisions about their lives. Their memoirs reconstruct the strong web of the family and communal relationships that sustained them, as they always have, during difficult times. These pages also depict individuals who adopted American business techniques and established substantial careers for themselves. But mostly they relate the bitter struggle of the 1930's which divided the ranks of the United Mine Workers. In this episode of union history, the United Anthracite Miners of Pennsylvania mounted a serious challenge to the UMW and the Glen Alden Coal Company in an attempt to rectify perceived abuses and restore economic well-being.

During the 1930's, as economic difficulties spread throughout the United States, the working people of Pennsylvania's anthracite region spoke loudly for two objectives. First, they were quite insistent that the limited work available at various mining operations be distributed equally among all people of the region. Secondly, many of them directed a bitter complaint against their long-time union, the UMW. A brief survey of the newspapers of the region during this period will confirm the importance of these two issues. What such a survey will not reveal, however, is the reason why anthracite miners and their families felt so strongly about job sharing and the inadequacy of the UMW. Such an understanding can only be gained by listening to the people of the region reconstruct the story of their lives and motives during the early decades of this century.

Central to the desires of anthracite people during the Great Depression was a fervent desire to share available work opportunities, to bring about what they called "job equalization." Equally as important was a demand that the United Mine Workers of America be replaced as their representative because of widespread corruption which enabled union leaders and coal operators to thrive at the expense of the rank and file. Indeed, this corrupt relationship was thought to be a major impediment to securing the ultimate goal of job equalization, since corrupt union officials favored some men over others in the distribution of work.

An understanding of the tremendous rank and file sentiment for these objectives is important because they were not the only alternatives mining people in this region had during hard times. Like all industrial workers they were concerned about exerting control at the workplace and, as described below, were frequently able to do it. Various labor organizers visited the region and attempted to organize men into "unemployed councils." Local politicians, fearing these councils as fertile ground for militancy, countered with the organization of "unemployed leagues." Community and religious leaders called continually for restraint. But despite urgings from both the left and the right, most miners in the northern fields went forward with their eyes riveted on union reform and the sharing of jobs; working-class protest, as one radical organizer admitted, was a creation of the region's own workers.[1]

Job equalization became the primary objective of anthracite people in response to increasingly hard times after 1930. In brief, the concept called for the even distribution of the mining and processing of hard coal among the various collieries owned by a company rather than their restriction to the one or two where the coal would be closest to the surface and, therefore, cheapest to obtain. To an extent, miners were challenging the company's right to control the production process and make management decisions solely on the basis of cost efficiency.

Throughout the hard-coal region, sporadic demands for job sharing emerged as unemployment climbed. In the Panther Valley area an equalization committee was formed by miners and local business and civic leaders to press the issue with the Lehigh Coal and Navigation Company. In August, 1933, over fifteen thousand men went on strike in the valley for "equalization of work time." The following year the Lithuanian

Catholic Action Convention in Girardsville adopted a resolution urging Franklin D. Roosevelt to compel operators to equalize work "even if no profits are realized and executive salaries are reduced." Similar demands came from the unemployed at the Loree Division of the Hudson Coal Company and from miners in Kingston and Shenandoah.[2]

Naturally, coal operators opposed such plans. They insisted that they be allowed to "concentrate" production at a few collieries where labor and production costs would be least. Such practices especially favored operations where coal did not have to be hoisted far or could be obtained with a minimum of blasting and rock removal. In fact, such practices had created unemployment so high by 1933 in such communities as Tamaqua, Coaldale, Nanticoke and Shenandoah that employment had dwindled to one-third of that of 1929. Despite recommendations by Secretary of Labor Frances Perkins for equalization, the operators argued strongly against the plan and claimed that it would erode further the already weak competitive position of anthracite coal relative to such newly emerging fuels as oil and gas.[3]

At some local collieries the men did not wait for political dialogue to settle the matter, but instituted plans of their own to allow greater numbers access to employment. At Glen Lyon, for instance, miners were able to overcome company opposition and establish a limit on the number of cars each man should load. If a miner was stationed in an area where coal was easily accessible, he would have a lower limit than men who could fill their cars only with a great deal of difficulty. As one miner recalled, "In most places it was five cars a day, but on some gangways it was four. If you were over the limit you would pay a fine." The goal of all this was, as the men themselves stated, to insure that each man got a fair day's wage and to "make the mines last longer for everyone."[4]

The entire issue of sharing the work reached a pivotal point in 1933 when the Roosevelt administration conducted hearings to establish National Recovery Administration (NRA) codes for the anthracite industry. John L. Lewis and the UMW had never been enthusiastic over equalization and were concerned primarily with higher wages and shorter hours. Indeed, one scholar has found that the UMW hierarchy was hopeful that Lewis' association with Roosevelt and the resulting prestige he would gain would mute the clamor for equalization and influence the hard-coal miners to put their faith in their union leaders.[5] While Thomas Kennedy, UMW national secretary, did call for equalization at the NRA hearings, it was a lukewarm endorsement made only after anthracite-region people had pressed their demands at the hearings in Washington. Representatives of the insurgent miners' organization, business associations, and local equalization committees all argued for a wider distribution of the available work so that miners could "maintain themselves, their families and their homes." [6]

The fragmentation of opinion among operators opposing equalization, union officials straddling the issue, and a working population demanding it prevented the consensus necessary for establishing an NRA code in the industry. While such a code would probably not have solved the economic problems of anthracite, the failure contributed to a further erosion of rank and file support for the UMW in the area and heightened the sympathy for a "dual union" which emerged in a wave of violence in 1933. [7]

Contemporaries who witnessed the bombings, beatings and violence which ravaged the northern anthracite fields between 1933 and 1936 tended to reduce the issue to one of the competing unions fighting for power. Central to the struggle was the formation of an insurgent union, the United Anthracite Miners of Pennsylvania, headed by Thomas Maloney. Leaders of the UAM were eventually convicted in a sensational trial during which the judge's car was bombed and Maloney was killed when someone mailed him a bomb. But the inspiration for the new UAM ran deeper than that portrayed in sensational news stories. [8] While some UAM leaders may have seen the UMW as simply a rival for influence, to its rank and file the old union of John L. Lewis had grown corrupt. While the anthracite industry may have suffered from the larger economic issue of cheaper, competitive fuels, the rank and file formulated the issue in more immediate terms: the UMW was self-serving and an obstacle to stable employment opportunities.

Interviews with men who participated in these events have revealed the low esteem in which the UMW was held. Chester Brozena, who was head of a UAM local at the Avondale Colliery, had asked for UMW help in 1934 because so many men were getting only two days' work a week. While no financial assistance was granted, the UMW did raise funds to repair the home of one of its officials, John Boylan, which had been dynamited by rival unionists. "This really threw everyone in an uproar," Brozena remembered. "Everyone started throwing chairs around and one said the hell with them [the UMW]." [9]

Dissatisfaction with the UMW was spreading. Joseph Krievak recalled that at Glen Lyon the union officials and the bosses worked together. It was the union officers who usually got the "better jobs," where coal was easier to mine. John Sarnoski, an immigrant miner from Poland, was furious that UMW officers would leave work for two weeks to attend conventions and still get paid for loaded cars. Such arrangements tempered considerably the protests of local UMW officials when they represented the men at their collieries who were blatantly cheated of their pay by companies that counted five loaded cars as only four. Bart Sheehan, a private detective hired by coal companies to investigate graft among mining bosses, told a federal investigation in 1933 that bosses regularly sold jobs and put men sympathetic to the UAM to work in locations where coal was more difficult to mine. And officials of large employers, such as Glen Alden Coal Company, had good reason to strengthen ties with the conservative UMW because they feared the more radical National Miners Union, which began speaking to their employees in 1933.[10]

The situation was clarified by a miner at Wanamie. Leonard Wydotis said that he supported the UAM because of the "collusion" between the UMW and the operators, and felt each miner should get a good day's pay and an "equal amount of work." Wydotis explained that it was difficult, however, to secure fair treatment and equalization if "men on the grievance committees were given the best jobs by the companies." Wydotis elaborated:

> The company and the union leaders went hand in hand. So if you didn't support them [UMW] you wouldn't have no jobs. Hell, the boss would go around and tell you who to vote for when we elected union officers. If you insulted the president of the local you wouldn't get a job no place, not even at another colliery.[11]

Miners not only perceived unscrupulous practices on the part of UMW leaders, but had definite ideas as to the origin of the problem. Invariably men attributed the growing rift between the union and the rank and file to the initiation of the checkoff system. In its 1930 contract the UMW had secured a "checkoff" system whereby the men's dues were paid from wages by the company directly to the unions and before the workers received their checks. The complaint of Thomas Maloney, UAM president, that their dues were being used for "pianos, pigs, and other articles" and his insistence that the system should be abolished angered UMW officials, whose union structure depended on this regular infusion of money.[12] Even more perceptive was the assessment of a Nanticoke miner. George Treski felt strongly that the UMW had begun to drift away from the ranks soon after 1930, when it no longer had to deal directly with the men to obtain dues payments. Treski reasoned:

> Before, you had to go to the union hall to pay your dues and then you would see the other members. If there were any problems you would thrash it out right there. After the checkoff system the union got the money but the people didn't go to the meetings and the union was doing whatever they wanted with the bosses. . . . Before, if you had a grievance you would holler at the union officials. After the checkoff you hardly saw them.[13]

6

Since UMW officials were supported directly by payments from companies through the checkoff, they could do nothing but support attempts of companies to destroy the UAM. In a remarkably candid recollection, William Everett, a superintendent for the Glen Alden Coal Company in the 1930's, explained just how effective company recrimination could be. In addition to denying UAM supporters jobs, Everett explained how he dealt with the Maloney supporters at work at his collieries. Recognizing that most of the men were for the UAM, he designed a plan to weaken certain "radical" UAM leaders. One foreman in particular, who spoke loudly for the insurgent union, was sent by Everett to another operation sixteen miles distant so that his journey to work would be more difficult. As he left, Everett warned him, "If I ever hear why you were transferred from any source, you gonna be out of a job." At another colliery he went to the home of a UAM leader, Mike Savilich, and told him to "tone down" his UAM activities. When the man's wife screamed at Everett, "He's not going to do a thing for you," Everett decided to punish him in a more subtle manner. The next day he placed a totally incompetent worker in Savilich's work gang in order to curtail his production. Everett explained his procedures this way: "You had to handle the people, manipulate them." [14]

Everett's attack on UAM leaders would often take the form of granting favors. At the Truesdale Colliery near Wilkes-Barre, he approached the UAM official at that site, Victor Matusa. Everett asked Matusa what made him a "radical." The miner responded that for years his father toiled at Truesdale at a "Catholic place"—a place where coal was so hard to remove it had to be carried as Christ carried his cross. The next day Matusa's father was moved to a better mining station and shortly thereafter Everett secured medical assistance for Matusa's son, who had a deformity. [15]

While the assault of the UAM upon the old union was necessary to obtain its larger goals of widespread and stable employment, a central question remains as to why the rank and file agitated for a sharing of work opportunities. Working-class leaders in the UMW had emphasized wages and hours, and, certainly, radical organizers were active in that area. It is true that UMW leaders had been discredited, but explanations of worker goals run deeper than simply that they were a reaction to those they may have disliked. A clue to rank and file motives can be glimpsed by looking briefly at the manner in which the insurgent unionists conducted their protest.

The salient feature of the UAM protest was its collective nature. Supporters of Thomas Maloney and the UAM attempted to curtail operations at various collieries by stopping work themselves and prohibiting

7

UMW sympathizers from getting to the collieries altogether, or by intimidation with dynamite. Invariably this was done in a communal way with not only the men but also the women and children of mining families participating.

Women were present everywhere in UAM activities. Several thousand joined the women's auxiliary. Led by spokeswomen such as Mary Bernatovich, the auxiliary secured the support for UAM activities from crucial unemployment councils in the area, and recruited speakers who could make appeals not only in English but in Polish and Lithuanian as well. Not surprisingly, when UAM leaders like Maloney were arrested in 1935 and held in contempt of court for violating a strike injunction, twelve of the ninety defendants were women.[16]

Women stood at the front ranks alongside their husbands, fathers and brothers in their attempt to stop UMW loyalists from going to work. During the 1935 violence women and children stoned men in the Hanover section of Nanticoke who were attempting to go to work. In Plymouth five women were arrested by State police for beating a miner on his way to work. Interestingly, the local press withheld the name of the victim but printed the names of the women. In fact, the arrest of five prompted an angry reaction from the UAM women's auxiliary, which charged that State police trying to maintain order in the region had abused women and declared that "women should cooperate with the new union." In Wilkes-Barre, shortly afterward, three miners were beaten by ten women who wrestled them to the ground. At Wanamie one evening, women were found "defying" State police who had been sent to the region to restore order. At high schools in Nanticoke and Wilkes-Barre, students organized support activities for the UAM. Over three hundred students called a strike at Nanticoke because several teachers had relatives working at Glen Alden collieries.[17] Communal protest reached a peak when mining families stoned the funeral procession of a miner who was killed while working during the 1935 strike, and filled the victim's open grave with tin cans. George Treski remembered that it was only the next day that the police had to be called to prevent the protestors from removing the body from the grave.[18]

It was no accident that the UAM protest, emerging as it did from the ranks of the mining communities, involved entire families and communities. Neither was it accidental that this protest ultimately sought a sharing of available work opportunities. For sharing and cooperation were central to the culture these mining people had established by the third decade of the twentieth century. And nowhere were these concepts better learned and employed than in the daily operation of family life. If the culture and lives of mining people had revolved around cooperative familial and

8

communal endeavors, it was reasonable to assume that, given the chance to express themselves, these people would attempt to apply the same strategy to solving larger economic problems. Whether these solutions were applicable to the sagging anthracite industry is not the question. They probably were not. But they were believed to be so by mining families and were pursued despite the retribution of company and union officials. The Glen Alden Coal Company, for instance, instituted a systematic campaign to evict UAM sympathizers from homes they rented from the company. This move evoked a stream of protest letters to federal officials, such as Frances Perkins, the Secretary of Labor, and President Franklin D. Roosevelt. Humble people sat down and wrote about the need for justice and the poverty they endured, and asked the President for help, as one put it, to "save my family." [19]

An understanding of this family-based culture and economy can be seen in the recollections of children who matured in that environment. The general pattern of their lives was clear. Childhood was followed by an early departure from school and an entry, as soon as possible, into the workplace. Earnings were turned over, regularly and routinely, to parents, and this support was rendered at least until marriage, but often for a lifetime.

Children moved into wage-earning jobs at a feverish pace. Antoinette Watchilla was raised in a family of five children. Characteristically, she entered a silk mill in Nanticoke at age twelve and brought her younger sisters into the mill as they reached adolesence. Her brother had already left school at age eleven to work for a farmer near Kingston. Viola Mazza hired out for housework by age twelve, while her sister went to a pants factory to sew. Marie Skovranski was born in 1914 and never left home. Since her mother was a dressmaker, Marie simply stayed home and assisted her. By the time she was fifteen, in 1916, Sophia Reakes had worked as a dressmaker, in a cigar mill, and as a cook in a mental hospital. Adelle Winarski left school following the sixth grade to seek employment in a silk mill.[20] Many young girls who did manage to finish high school left the coal regions immediately to obtain housework from wealthier families in the New York City area. Irene Wieczorek claimed that being Polish gave one such a good reputation as a houseworker that employment came easily. Stacia Treski, who temporarily left Nanticoke for New York in the early 1930's, was able to send sixty per cent of her twenty-five-dollar monthly income to her parents.[21]

Young men, of course, followed the same pattern as their sisters, except that they worked first around the mines in breakers, or as "nippers" opening doors for loaded coal cars and spragging them when they had to be stopped. Underground work, usually as a laborer to a contract miner, did not begin much before the age of eighteen. Typical was the case of Steve Stashar, who entered the employ of the mines in Glen Lyon at the age of sixteen and helped support his family for seven years until his younger brother was old enough to enter the mines and his sister could go to New York to perform housekeeping services. [22]

The fact that familial obligations dictated wage sharing and entry into work life in the first place was reinforced by the dependence on kin for access to available jobs. This process was crucial for those from abroad. For instance, Lillian Niziolek's father came from Poland to the Susquehanna Coal Company because a brother already in Nanticoke secured an opening for him. Lillian's father in turn brought six cousins and nephews to the same mines. Not infrequently sons would labor with their fathers, as Stanley Salva did in Glen Lyon; or women would talk to a "floor lady" in the silk mill about work for their sisters. When work was scarce, particularly during a strike, workers would move to other regions to live with kin and earn wages, usually returning when work resumed. [23]

While it is clear that families and kin assisted each other, it should not be assumed that this was done in a perfunctory manner. While family tensions existed and obligations generated inevitable pressures, family members—especially children—felt a strong obligation to assist their kin and frequently did so with a deep sense of purpose. The basis for this attitude seemed to be a widespread assumption on the part of adolescents that their parents had worked hard and struggled all their lives and deserved all the help progeny could render. Stanley Salva explained that it was expected that as soon as one was old enough and strong enough, he went into the mines and earned wages. He emphasized, "That's what I wanted." Helen Klish left school after grade eleven and began working in a Nanticoke restaurant because she used to see her mother worrying about the mortgage on the family home and felt she was "old enough to owe her that much." [24] As a young girl of twelve in 1918, Mary Yukenevich toiled in a tailor shop "because I wanted to help my mother and father." Antoinette Watchilla revealed that she could not concentrate on school "when we needed money in the house." Because she admired her mother for working hard without complaining, she felt compelled to earn wages and turn them over. Virginia Vida and her brothers helped their parents in Nanticoke because they "felt sorry" for them for laboring so hard. [25] And Helen Hosey summed up the feeling when she explained: "You took care of one another. You never questioned it. In our family we never expected anything in return. It was the honor that we had. The trust—that's why we all felt so close to each other. There was no house divided here." [26]

The strong feelings evoked by struggling parents in their working-class children not only led to a deep-seated desire to assist the family of origin, but also carried over into a widespread drive to establish families of their own; life was to be carried on within a context of marriage and the family. Tied closely to their industrial economy, working-class community and kin, working-class children saw adulthood in the 1920's and 1930's as an extension of their familial and communal culture, not as a departure, although a marriage of one's own did represent something of an independent thrust. Daughters and sons grew to emulate their parents and maintain the system of sharing and assisting. Jule Znaniecki respected her mother immensely for raising her despite the tragedy of losing three children to the flu, and she wanted to raise a family of her own. Stacia Feddock detailed how her mother struggled to raise five dollars for a First Communion dress and then revealed that her own life would have been "unthinkable" without a child. Another woman exclaimed: "That was the social thing to do. You didn't say you would get married and not have children. That wasn't the pattern. I'm glad there was a pattern." [27]

Indeed, grandchildren themselves could often represent an additional contribution on the part of children to their admired parents. Marie Skovranski and her husband revealed how her father rejoiced at the birth of her son because the infant replaced, in the grandfather's eyes, Marie's brother who had died at age seven. [28]

But while marriage was eagerly pursued, working-class family ties and patterns of carrying and assisting each other were not discarded; children continued to care for their parents, especially as they reached old age. After Stacia Feddock's father suffered a serious stroke, she would sit with him daily and listen to stories about his life in Poland. Even when Virginia Vida reached middle age she never had a day that she did not visit her mother. Several children confessed to their inability to move from the coal regions as they matured because they felt obligated to remain near their parents. Many took their parents into their own homes or moved in with them to offer care during old age. Vincent Znaniecki's brother actually built his parents a home. Marriages were postponed past age forty and even fifty so that care could be extended for elderly parents. Marie Siegley visited her parents every day until they died. "After they died I don't even remember the times," she said. "It was like a blackout." [29]

But it would be a mistake to conclude that reciprocity did not exist in parent-child relationships. Parents knew all along that they would need both the material and emotional support of their children, and provided both discipine and valuable services which would insure child support in subsequent years. Parents were not about to leave the possibility of child assistance to chance or sentiment alone. When the situation called for it they were not averse to insisting upon child labor and earnings. When Marie Skovranski was in the eighth grade her brother became ill and her mother asked her to leave school and help care for him. After her father died of a heart attack, Virginia Vida's mother "made the kids work." At age sixteen Virginia went out to do housework and baby-sit.[30]

Often a child's work efforts were directed toward small, family business pursuits, which were established throughout such industrial regions as the anthracite coal fields. Arlene Golobek's parents opened up a small grocery store in Nanticoke, hoping that the business would ultimately enable her father to leave the mines. Arlene was kept busy seven days a week in the enterprise cleaning mushrooms and helping in the store. Eleanor Ostrowski left school after the ninth grade and worked in her parents' store.[31]

Children, of course, did not always appreciate strict parental discipline or the demand that they enter the workplace at an early age and relinquish their wages to their parents. Arguments occurred frequently. Several young men ran away from home because they had to work for their fathers. Discipline was often enforced with a strap. One woman resented her father's attempt to regulate her dating patterns and influence her choice of a marriage partner. Sophia Reakes described how children in her family had to kiss their parents' hands and ask for forgiveness before they went to Holy Communion in the Catholic church.[32] Clearly parents felt that the family could not act in concert to meet economic exigencies over a lifetime without a certain degree of discipline.

But discipline was not all that parents had to give. They also proved indispensable in providing housing, a valuable commodity in the coal regions, even after children had been married. If unable to afford housing of their own, as was often the case, young couples moved in with their parents for as long as several years. Stacia Feddock's parents saved feverishly for a home and then acquired a second one next door so they would be able to give each of their two daughters a home of her own. One woman reported that she and her husband moved in with her parents whenever he was out of work. Another man revealed how he lived with his mother-in-law for a while after marriage, and then built a home of his own on a lot he inerhited from his mother. Regina Haranzy's father received a home from his parents, which they built on the back of their lot; the parents continued to reside on the front part of the property. When one miner got sick and could no longer repair his home, he asked his son-in-law to take it from him for one dollar and keep it in repair. While houses were often built very cheaply by family members themselves, the widespread sharing of housing resources within family systems underscored the intricate workings of the family economy.[33]

Despite a general pattern of sharing responsibilities within these working-class families, some members exerted more authority than others. Certainly males exerted some authority and discipline: unable to derive status from their menial jobs, it might be expected they would seek status at home. But it is necessary to point out that both their status and authority at home were usually secondary to their wives'. Women were simply pre-eminent at home and assumed a wide range of responsibilities, including management of family finances. In many instances it was coal-region housewives who decided to initiate small, family businesses or purchase a home. This does not seem surprising since women generally possessed the most accurate knowledge of family financial resources, which were regularly turned over to them by husbands and children. As Helen Hosey (and nearly every respondent in this study) explained, "My mother always handled the money; my father never even opened his pay envelope." [34]

Women took their responsibility seriously and performed their role aggressively. When Sophie Reakes spent one dollar of her earnings on a petticoat before turning her wages over, her mother threatened to throw her out of the home. Women would frequently risk social ostracism and enter local taverns on payday before husbands had an opportunity to drink away modest earnings. Many miners never entered taverns at all, but those who did posed a threat to family harmony and economy. Indeed, one woman recalled hiding wives in her family's store who feared additional beatings from drunk spouses. [35]

Not only did family members perform prescribed roles and share, when necessary, their wages and housing, their collective approach to family needs extended to others in the working-class enclave. Because the gathering of food was a continuous process, it required participation from extended kin and neighbors as well as from parents and children. Men would prepare smoked sausage and women would make sauerkraut, can fruits and vegetables, and store them in cold cellars. Neighbors would swap foods for greater variety. Feathers were peeled from ducks for pillows and blankets. And everyone picked coal to enhance winter supplies. [36]

On religious holidays extended kin would gather for dinner and visitations. Christmas celebrations were especially remembered as familial and communal affairs in which traditional customs that stemmed from eastern Europe predominated. While economic realities elevated the internal status of the mother, it was the father, acting as titular head of the household, who passed the sacred wafer ("oplatek" in Polish) around the table on Christmas eve. It was the soothing influence of tradition and nostalgia that muted the realities of life and work and made the world appear as it should, and not as it was, during holidays. Some children even recalled that they prayed for familial and communal goals, such as better homes for their parents and kin.[37]

Communal sharing meant, at times, an even greater commitment. Many women actually raised the children of female neighbors who had died. Mildred Zejack was raised by an aunt after her mother died in childbirth. Frequently, old brothers and sisters raised younger ones when parents passed away. Viola Mazza's parents took in a neighbor's daughter of five when her mother died. Even with ten children of her own, Lillian Niziolek's mother would bring food to neighborhood women who had given birth. Sophie Reakes recalled that even though her mother had eleven children, she took in another who was orphaned. During weddings and funerals large numbers of neighbors would gather and give food and comfort. Chester Brozena revealed that during funerals neighbors would bring hams, care for smaller children, and even take time from work to sit in the homes of the bereaved and lend emotional support. Men would pick extra coal for neighbors who were unable to work.[38] And every mining family relied on the cooperative spirit of the local storekeeper who allowed it to buy "on the book." One miner revealed,

> The fellow that should have a monument is the small storekeeper; he is the guy that kept you on the book. Otherwise you'd never won a strike here. . . . When a strike came—why he just kept on taking on his book and you didn't pay him until you started back to work. If he demanded his money when it was due, you couldn't have survived.[39]

Certainly the working-class family and community should not be romanticized. Factionalism in the ranks of miners represented by the UMW and the UAM cannot be ignored and tensions between parents and children were frequent enough; limits to cooperation existed. But the results of this study indicate that a persistent pattern of sharing and cooperation was rigorously enforced. It was pursued with such rigor, in fact, that deviations from proper role fulfillment could upset a very tenuous harmony and lead to exceptionally high incidences of manic depression and dementia praecox.

As the economic difficulties of the anthracite region mounted after 1930 and as the miners sought for ways to solve their problems, it should not be surprising that the miners turned to such a solution as job equalization. They were willing to share the available work because cooperation and sharing were the means by which they had always met the exigencies of industrial life. Above all else their behavior and perceptions were rooted in the institution which emerged at the intersection of traditional and industrial cultures—the family economy. They vigorously attacked the United Mine Workers with all their collective resources—men, women and children—because it stood in the way of achieving their fundamental goal of sharing. While the United Anthracite Miners may have lost its ultimate battle to an entrenched union and the powerful coal companies, the quest for cooperation was genuine, was participated in widely, and was shaped not by repressive companies, big government, or even an industrial workplace, but from below in the intimate workings of the family culture. And in the 1936 anthracite contract, the UMW finally included—though never implemented—a statement in support of equalization.

What was most significant in the struggle of anthracite-region people in the 1930's was the powerful statement they made about life's priorities. Labor historians who reduce working-class behavior to a product of the workplace and whose major concern is with who exercises greater control on the production line, have unnecessarily reduced the framework in which worker behavior should be analyzed. Industrial workers were not simply, as Marxist historians would suggest, tied to the material realities of the workplace. Their views were not, moreover, inherently radical nor were they moderated only by governmental intrusion. There were some radical workers, of this we can be sure. But the attitudes of most workers were rooted, ultimately, in the loving concern which united both family and neighborhood and also in the tensions which pervaded these relationships. If industrial managers were unable to instill the degree of discipline on the line that they would have liked, it may have been because a stronger dose of discipline was administered at home; the scheme of mutual obligation between parents and children was indelibly impressed on workers. The family economy suffered traumas to be sure, but this seemed only to underscore how seriously family members took their responsibilities. They did not forget their mutual responsibility when the time came to speak out.

Footnotes

[1] Steve Nelson, James R. Barrett, and Rob Ruk, *Steve Nelson: An American Radical* (Pittsburgh, 1981), pp. 160-73.

[2] *United Mine Workers Journal*, XLV (June 15, 1934), p. 14; (May 1, 1934), p. 13. *Wilkes-Barre Record*, Nov. 21, 1933, p. 14; *New York Times*, Aug. 21, 1933, p. 27; Nov. 18, 1933, p. 7.

[3] "Report on Operations of the Lehigh Navigation Coal Company, Aug. 8, 1938," Lehigh Coal and Navigation Company Records, MG 31, Pennsylvania Historical and Museum Commission (PHMC), Harrisburg. This report admitted that labor has learned to act as a unit in resisting efforts of the management to decrease costs. *UMW Journal*, XLV (Jan. 15, 1934), p. 8; May 1, 1934, p. 4. *Wilkes-Barre Record,* Nov. 18, 1933, p. 14; Nov. 22, 1933, p. 1.

⁴ Joe Sudol interview by John Bodnar, March 10, 1981 tape recording (PHMC); Stanley Salva interview by Bodnar, March 19, 1981 (PHMC); Ben Grevera and Anthony Piscotty interview by Bodnar, March 24, 1981 (PHMC).

⁵ Douglass K. Monroe, "A Decade of Turmoil: John L. Lewis and the Anthracite Miners, 1926-1936," (unpublished Ph.D. dissertation, Georgetown University, 1976), pp 215-30.

⁶ *Wilkes-Barre Record*, Nov. 18, 1933, pp. 1, 14; *UMW Journal*, XLVII (Aug. 8-15, 1936), p. 5; XLIV (Dec. 1, 1933), pp. 3-4, 8. See Pierce Williams to Harry L. Hopkins, Jan. 10, 1935, Harry Hopkins Papers, Franklin D. Roosevelt Library.

⁷ An indication of the UMW's lack of interest in the rank and file goal of equalization came at the 1935 UMW convention for the anthracite region. The only resolutions passed at the convention were against the United Anthracite Miners, a rival group, and "pusher bosses." No mention was made of equalization. See *UMW Journal*, XLVI (Dec. 15, 1935), p. 3.

⁸ Thomas Maloney, head of the United Anthracite Miners, was arrested along with other leaders of the union for contempt in his failure to honor a strike injunction. Thousands of miners encircled the courthouse during the ensuing trial, which was broadcast on local radio. See *Wilkes-Barre Record*, April 11, 1936, p. 1; Feb. 8, 1935, p. 17; Feb. 11, 1935, p. 1; March 5, 1935, p. 1. "Investigations of Reports Concerning Conduct of State Police in Strike Zone, May 6, 1935," Records of the Pennsylvania State Police, RG 30, Box 3, PHMC.

⁹ Chester Brozena interview by Bodnar, April 15, 1981, tape recording (PHMC).

¹⁰ Joseph Krievak interview by Bodnar, March 19, 1981; John Sarnoski interview by Bodnar, March 10, 1981; Vincent Znaniecki interview by Bodnar, Feb. 5, 1981; Stanley Salva interview, March 19, 1981; all interviews tape recorded (PHMC).

¹¹ Leonard Wydotis interview by Bodnar, March 3, 1981 tape recording (PHMC). By 1933 the union local at Wanamie to which Wydotis belonged was so strong for the UAM that John L. Lewis revoked its charter; see *Wilkes-Barre Record*, Nov. 21, 1932, p. 20.

¹² *Wilkes-Barre Record*, Nov. 18, 1933, p. 1.

¹³ George and Stacia Tresniowski interview by Bodnar, March 3, 1981, tape recording (PHMC). See also Grevera and Piscotty interview, March 24, 1981.

¹⁴ William Everett interview by Bodnar, March 29, 1981, tape recording (PHMC).

¹⁵ *Ibid.*

¹⁶ For account of women participating in anthracite labor protest in earlier times see Victor Greene, *The Slavic Community on Strike* (Notre Dame, 1968) and Michael Novak, *The Guns of Lattimer* (New York, 1978). For an account of unemployment councils in the region see Nelson, Barrett and Ruck, *Steve Nelson: American Radical.*

¹⁷ *Wilkes-Barre Record*, Feb. 12, 1935, p. 13; March 1, 1935, p. 26. "Industrial Disturbance, Anthracite Coal District," Strike Reports, Pennsylvania State Police Records, RG 30 (PHMC).

¹⁸ *Wilkes-Barre Record*, March 18, 1935, p. 13; March 26, 1935, p. 13. George and Stacia Treski interview, March 3, 1981. "Arrest for Dynamiting in Luzerne County," Strike Reports, Pennsylvania State Police Records, Box 3.

¹⁹ See Peter Gerko (Plymouth, Pennsylvania) to Franklin D. Roosevelt, March 24, 1935; Lana Gorgus to Franklin D. Roosevelt, March 25, 1935; "Mine Workers of Wanamie" to Franklin D. Roosevelt, Feb. 20, 1935, Federal Mediation and Conciliation Service Dispute File, RG 280, National Archives. Glen Alden President William Inglis sent a telegram to the U.S. Department of Labor stating that he planned to go ahead with the eviction program because UAM sympathizers had interfered with production and the implementation of the contract between the company and UMW. Evidence also existed that companies like Glen Alden were violating the contract themselves by hiring independent gangs of labor (1932) and paying them below union scale to mine coal. Most men felt this was taking jobs away from their communities. See William Inglis to Hugh Kerwin, telegram, Feb. 23, 1935; Stephen Matyleurs to Frances Perkins, June 2, 1935, Federal Mediation and Conciliation Service Dispute File.

[20] Antoinette Watchilla interview by Angela Staskavage, July 2, 1977; Helen Knepp interview by Bodnar, Sept. 16, 1978; Viola Mazza interview by Staskavage, Sept. 18, 1977; Sophia Reakes interview by Staskavage, July 13, 1977; Adelle Winarski interview by Staskavage, Aug. 1, 1977; Irene Wieczorek interview by Bodnar, March 26, 1981.

[21] Irene Wieczorek interview, Nov. 26, 1977; Stacia Treski interview, March 3, 1981.

[22] Steve Stashak interview by Bodnar, March 19, 1981; Peter Byczkowski interview by Bodnar, May 18, 1981; Steve Gotcha interview by Bodnar, May 18, 1981; Joseph Sudol interview by Bodnar, March 3, 1981; Joseph Molski interview by Bodnar, March 4, 1981. All interviews tape recorded (PHMC).

[23] Lillian Niziolek interview by Kenneth Hughes, July 13, 1977; Joseph Krivak interview by Bodnar, March 19, 1981; Stanley Salva interview by Bodnar, March 19, 1981; Vincent Znaniecki interview by Bodnar, Feb. 5, 1981; Viola Mazza interview, Sept. 18, 1977; Betty Hoskins interview by Staskavage, Jan. 18, 1978. All interviews are tape recorded (PHMC).

[24] Stanley Salva interview, March 19, 1981; Helen Klish interview, Sept. 19, 1977.

[25] Mary Gill interview by Staskavage, March 25, 1977; Antoinette Watchilla interview, July 12, 1977; Virginia Vida interview, Dec. 6, 1977.

[26] Helen Hosey interview by James Rodechko, July 21, 1977: tape recording (PHMC).

[27] Jule Znaniecki interview by Staskavage, July 7, 1977; Stacia Feddock interview by Shirley Donio, August 27, 1977; Marie Siegley interview by Staskavage, Jan. 11, 1978. All interviews tape recorded (PHMC).

[28] Marie Skovranski interview by Staskavage, Jan. 16, 1978, tape recording (PHMC).

[29] Stacia Feddock interview, Aug. 27, 1977; Irene Wieczorek interview, Nov. 26, 1977; Sophie Reakes interview, July 13, 1977; Pearl C. interview by Bodnar, March 17, 1981; Marie Siegley interview, Jan. 11, 1978, tape recording (PHMC).

[30] Marie Skovranski interview, Jan. 16, 1978; Virginia Vida interview, Dec. 6, 1977; Joseph Sudol interview, March 3, 1981; Stanley Salva interview, March 19, 1981; Joseph Molski and Leonard Wydotis interview, March 10 1981.

[31] Arlene Godolek interview, Dec. 11, 1977; Eleanor Ostrowski interview, Nov. 11, 1977; Sophie Reakes interview, July 3, 1977.

[32] *Ibid*, Sophie Wojcik interview, by Staskavage, Sept. 14, 1977; Stella K. interview by Bodnar, May 8, 1981.

[33] See Stacia Feddock interview, Aug. 27, 1977; Marie Skovranski interview, Jan. 16, 1978; Vincent Znaniecki interview, Feb. 5, 1981; Virginia Vida interview, Dec. 6, 1977.

[34] *Ibid.,* Viola Mazza interview, Sept. 17, 1977.

[35] Arlene Gobolek interview, Dec. 11, 1977; Sophie Reakes interview, July 17, 1977; Helen Klish interview, Sept. 17, 1977; Steve Gotcha interview, May 18, 1981; John Sarnoski interview, March 10, 1981.

[36] Joseph Molski interview, March 3, 1981; Leonard Wydotis, March 3, 1981; Helen Klish, September 17, 1977; Arlene Golobek, Dec. 11, 1977.

[37] Sophie Wojcik interview, Sept. 14, 1977; Helen Klish interview, Sept. 17, 1977; Virginia Vida interview, Dec. 6, 1977; Marie Siegley interview, Jan. 11, 1978.

[38] Mildred Weiss interview, Aug. 23, 1977; Lillian Niziolek interview, Sept. 13, 1977; Joseph Krivak interview, March 19, 1981.

[39] Chester Brozena interview, March 15, 1981. Although it was illegal, even tavern owners extended credit during strikes or hard times.

17

Newcomers

Louis Micocci, right, visits his family in Italy, 1915.

Louis Micocci

Much of the Nanticoke area and the entire Wyoming Valley were set-
tled by newcomers from abroad. One such individual was Louis Micocci,
who emigrated from Italy. He retells not only his experiences in the Old
World but of his association with the Susquehanna Coal Company.

MICOCCI: I born April 7, 1895 in a little town about forty miles south of
Rome. The town is supposed to be an old town according to the history
what we have. Existed about thirty-five, forty years before Christ. And
the population, mostly farmer, but they no live on the farm. They live in
the town. And every morning, and the sun rises, sometimes even before
the sunrise, they go on out to the fields, some of the land even about
three, four mile away. And they work all day, and then they come back
in the evening and usually nobody stay out of the town. At one time, not
my time but before me, there was two doors, big gates. And they were
locked at a certain time of the night, because there used to be what you
could call a "brigandi"—in other words he's a thief. They go around
steal anything they could ever steal. Very few people has a gun, except a
couple of wealthy people or something like that. The town is a very nice
town to live in, clean air, no industry which you get smoke or anything.
And a lot of people will come to pass their vacation during the summer.
Looked like my family been in Gaviano for century back, because my
grandfather, I remember. I don't remember my great grandfather, but I
know he was born and raise in Gaviano also. So go back, very many
years back, the family come around from Gaviano. That actually might
be one thousand years back, God know, what was, you know, where
they came from. Some are now there on my mother's side. The name is
Delmonte. They walk to the fields, a few—some a little more than other,
used to use a donkey, riding on a donkey. And the donkey was used for
more than one purpose, riding back and forth, and also using it to trans-
port, as a transportation for the harvest in the fields that they were loading on the top of the donkey, and they bring him home. You have a regular place where you put you grain, wheat or corn or oats. That was the
most of three grain which was raising on the territory. And they used to
use some beans, some potatoes, but the grain is wheat, corn, and oats,
that's the three thing what are very big used. And the land was cultivated, one year they cultivated, they put in corn, next year they put the
wheat, third year you put in your oats. And that's the way you rent this
land. There's a big owner of the land, that's what he give to these farmers. For three years, you the one that's responsible to cultivate that. And
then you divided up at harvest time, either two to one or three to one,
more or less.

The farmer get someplace they are calling it two-thirds, get two-thirds and the owner get one. Someplace they even have some cash you have to pay, maybe five dollars cash a year for the three years. At the end of the three years, the owner can take that land out of you and give to somebody else. There's no such thing you have that for years on top of years. Sometimes when you are the farmer they don't care much about the next three years. Usually they don't like it the production. That's how you lived, everything like that. Some of these poor farmer there, they didn't never make enough to buy whole suit in one time. There be one year there be enough to buy the coat, next year maybe they have enough to buy the pants, next year might have enough to buy the shoes. I mean, not very many could buy the whole suit in one time.

My mother and father were not the poorest. They were in the middle, what you want to call the middle class. They have this own house, they have this own place where they storage the grain, they have a little room where they can put a couple of cows. But this cow wasn't for milk or anything, more likely for commercial, in other words, they buy a small cow, they raise it, and then at a certain time, they selling and make a few dollars. Like I said now, my father built a new home the time I was born. That means by eighty-three, eighty-four years back. And the cost of that was fifteen hundred lire. That equal over three hundred dollars. But they only have one thousand lire, and the five hundred they don't have it. And my father don't want to have no debts. So he don't want to sign a—what do you call them?—a note to nobody. And my poor mother will go crazy because was very important to finish the house the way they supposed to be, to spend the other five hundred lire. So she went to one rich man which have the money, and she told him the situation. Her husband won't sign no note. And this man told her, I don't need no note from you, here's the five hundred lire. And my mother was happy that she know very well that within a year or two she would have the five hundred lire back to him, which they did. But then my father, he was still poor. Other people would come in America, he wanted to come in America. And then my father when he stay, he didn't want to stay too long away from the family, he came back after one season, 1906. About six, seven months, he was here. He worked around whatever they can find in what they would dig and make the road. Whatever construction he found. They didn't even know write and reading, anything, mother and father. Well, some place they were living [as] boarder[s] with some other people in houses, but some of these construction [workers], especially railroad, they were building shanty, big shanty [to live in]. And they have a coach, maybe on two floor, two level of coach. They were living there, and they were cooking themselves, but they buying his own dishes, pots and pans, not too many, whatever. They were cooking himself in order to save money. Because you stay with somebody in houses, you pay two, three dollars a month to do that. And that's all you was getting, maybe three dollars a month. So they, in order to save money—and they sent home the money, whenever they have ten, twenty, thirty dollars, they would send it back to the family. My father don't want to stay the second year, so he come back home in the fall. But three years after 1908, he want to come again and he did.

My mother said, "Well then, why don't you take the whole family there?" So, well I don't like to have a family in America. OK, he came back the second time. In 1909, he want to come back again for the third time, he did. He did come back a third time.

Q: To Pennsylvania again?

MICOCCI: Yeah, always around here in Pennsylvania between Nanticoke to Wilkes-Barre. But during the winter between 1909 and 1910, in fact I think it was January 1910, he lost an eye in the job. You know, the picking ice, piece of ice hit one of the eye. And he lost an eye, and no compensation, nothing, he had to pay everything on his own. When the March 1910 and the news come, he lost an eye, my mother said, get ready boys, we all going in America. I was the oldest one and the one that was writing the letter. Now I was fifteen years old. My mother said, "Dear husband, look around for a house, because we come to America. If you answer yes, I going to come. If you answer no, I going to come just the same." So he had no choice, and my mother used to be one of those determined woman which means what she said. She was a very intelligent woman. And the man who's reading the letter to my father, he said, "Better answer yes because I know your wife just as well you do, and she going to be here with the children without any problems." So my father said yes, and the same time he find a little house, was a company house that they used to have. They call them a company house. And we left the hometown in August 17. We got to Mocanaqua on September 3. It was a rainy day, and September 3 was on a Sunday. And we looked for a family from our hometown. I didn't even know any, but my mother know it and remembered Tiberi. The fellow named Tiberi family in Nanticoke. But my father went to Scranton to meet us. He thought we come into the Lackawanna Station. But then when he got there, they told him the ship was quaranteened—do you know what I mean? You can't get out of the ship; there was something, some disease on the ship, and you can't get out until this be over. But anyhow, then you don't know what to do anymore. And he didn't come home for three days after we were already in Mocanaqua. In beginning wish we didn't come here to stay, period. We don't like it, we like to stay to make money. Then go back to Italy and enjoy it. That's what we waited for, the whole family. My mother too. Up to 1915 when we move to Chester, then she change her mind. Well, what happened, the coal—the mines—the West End Coal Company was working one of the best coal you can get. It was working wonderful every day. And we went to work every day, six days a week, nine hours a day. And we were making a little money. I was working, my next brother was working, and my father was working. We even fill the bag with coal, we take them home during the summer. And we make a pile of coal enough for the winter. We never bought a ton of coal. But we do that before we go to work. Then we break it. When you go home at night we break it. So for five years we never bought a ton of coal. But then in 1915, during March, they started to slow down. Was work only two, three days a week. And we don't like that and we all—we were out of work. We have, by accident, we have a letter from a lady, a woman from Chester, who was my father's godchild. She had a old address of my father. But it was really wrong address. But anyhow, the letter came in Nanticoke, and the mailman bring this letter to every Italian house. Nobody can read and nobody can understand what the letter was all about. Finally, she got to one house, it was a neice to my mother and father. She decide to open, she decide to open that letter. When open that letter, the way the letter was written, she know it belong to my father. She know the woman that wrote this letter. And so, I happen on a Sunday, I came in Nanticoke, and she gave me this letter. The letter said, you not work there, we have a lot of work over here. So that's why we move into Chester. Then my mother said, "You better go to see what's all about." So they sent me to Chester, and when I got there, I got on a Sunday, it was June 21, 1915. And then Monday I was working [at a] place where they used to make a locomotive.

I was the oldest brother. Then I had an extra brother, two years younger, Virginio, and then I have a sister, and then I have one baby brother.

But I went back to Italy on September the 3, 1915. I was already in uniform, soldier uniform after the war broke out. I was afraid that after the war my family would go back home in time and I couldn't go back because I would have been punished, treated like a deserter. And so I don't like that. And my mother was pretty smart. I said, "Mama, what should I do?" And she said, "Whatever you think is, I don't say go, I don't say stay." I said, "If I don't go, then you people go home and I can't come with you 'cause I going to get put in jail." And so I didn't know that she was pretty smart. In other words, she didn't want to take no responsibility. I decide to go. I said, well, I was thinking the war was already three, four months old. Take about six months. Everybody won't go to war, how long the war can last? One year? Nobody figure it last the one year. I was forty-two months in the war, almost four years. My father and mother are still in Chester. They spent all the money buying the property in the territory of Gaviano. They sent money to my brother who was there. He's the one who has managed our money and everything else. Because then when you have this land, you have to have somebody to collect from these farmers who are working and all. You have to administer, in other words. So you see, we were like a, what you call it, "little rich people." Then my mother was thinking, it was better to stay in America and forget that. You're going to sell it, what you get some kind of income out of that. And anytime you want to see it, you sell it. That's what we did. Not all at one time, but within a few years after. Until I come back here, we had everything. While I was there, I was using some of the income because Italian soldier only get ten cents a day. What are you going to do with ten cents a day? OK, I was a corporal, I was get fourteen cents. Then I was a major-corporal, nineteen cents a day. I went back to Chester after the war. My family was there. I come back here with my wife and a little daughter, a little girl, two months old, two and a half months old. But those day in Chester, I went back to work with the Sun Oil where my brother was then. But it was very low pay, thirty-five cents an hour. I didn't, can't hardly make a living, and I didn't like much charity either. I didn't like all those smoke, I was losing my appetite and everything. I don't feel too good. And so we had a lot of relatives in Nanticoke from our hometown. And so we come back to Nanticoke, me and my brother-in-law, we both come back, come in Nanticoke. And so we got job with the Susquehanna Coal Company. And I was there, I was in a labor gang, you know, with the labor gang means you fix the track where the mine car go. You fix anything has to be wrong, you have to clean the snow when the snow come, general labor. You have to make pieces of track, little track for miner cars all the time. But meantime, the carpenter boss is looking for painters. So he went to my boss, the labor boss, says, "Do you know anybody on your gang that is a painter, who know how to paint?" He says, "I don't know, there's one man there, he said, he's got a lot of paint on his clothes." And he come over to me and said, "Do you know how to paint?" I says, "Sure." Now, I don't want to be on the labor gang at all, I hate the labor gang. And I says, sure. I was too quick—I didn't even hesitate. And I don't know anything about it, tell you the truth. He says, "Wait here for the brush come in; as soon as the brush come in, I going to call you." Sure enough, on Columbus Day, October 12, 1921, in the morning I went to the labor gang, and the foreman said he wants to see you. It was the name of the carpenter boss. Well, I thought, I won't be alone, there'll be another painter usually. The other one know how to paint, I learn from him. I was painting a powder house in 1925. It was a big job. So three days before, a strike was coming, and I know they were hiring people to another colliery. I went over there, I took a day off from the colliery, went over there, and I got the job. But I couldn't stay two, three days away from this job. If they find out they would fire me. But after one day, nobody noticed and then the next day a fellow, a friend of mine, was work there in the powder house for this contract. I said, tell the boss I want to go down to Chester pick up my family, my family in Chester. Well, it wasn't true, that was just what I told them. So I work all the strike; I was working mixing cement, anything, anything. That's what I was doing because as long as I was working—I have a family I was just starting, I have two baby, I have twins. That was my wife, the first was twins, a boy and a girl. And they were born in 1925 in April; this was in the fall. And even we were short of coal; sometime I had to take time off for that, to go pick the coal in these bag, you know, these rope bag. Pick coal was pleasure for two children, I mean because it was their situation, I mean, that's what I did the whole strike.

Well, some of them scatter round all over; they went in different state, different place. Others just thought they had something in the bank, they ought to eat what they have, using the reserve if they have it. They try to do the best they could; what can you do, I mean, in a situation like that? It was a lot of time away, it was kind of tough. People those days they were working a piece of land, they were making what you call home-grow garden and all and everything. I was doing the same thing. Tomatoes, we have tomatoes, broccoli, red beets and carrots and all these things. I had a few chicken in the backyard for eggs and everything. I mean, you always can do if you have ambition. You always manage to make a living.

Q: How did these grievance committees work at these collieries?

MICOCCI: Well, the grievance committee would—the way I understood they were working it, you think where you working you need something and the bosses don't want to agree with you or the boss—then you go to the grievance committee 'cause otherwise the boss can't deal with every man. You go to grievance committee and report and tell them what's it all about. Then the grievance committee supposed to go to the boss, and try to straighten out or try to let this man get what belong to him. Some of these miners claim they were short in the car, they load maybe twenty-five cars and they only get pay for twenty. Sometimes they report that to the grievance committee. I know some of the grievance committee they do wrong. 'Cause one time I complain, I have a spray, bring the spray, and using the spray I would like to get more money. Besides that, with the spray you're getting all the fume of the spray and everything is more or less entitled—you entitle more money. So I went to the union find out which was the rate, what rate was for the spray. But the painters, they didn't never painted before; they didn't never schedule the rate—the colliery, each job has a rate. Well, I say, OK. But they said, we going to try to find out. That's all I said, nothing help. But the president of this local, the same night he went to the superintendent and tell so many lie about me, I was bitching. I was complain[ing] about it [the lying], and a lot of things, and I only ask the question [about the rates], nothing else. And the superintendent got really mad. The next morning I was wait for the superintendent, I have to ask something. When he come, he was like wild. I said to him, "Mr. Weinich, I just went over there ask them what's the rate if I using the spray." He said, "No, you don't, you say so many thing. If you don't like the job, why don't you quit?" I said, "Well, if I don't do the right thing, why don't you fire me?" Oh, I was mad. But then during the day he find out what type a man was this "super"—this president of the local was.

Q: How long do you work now with the Susquehanna Coal Company?

MICOCCI: Well, I work from 1920 until 1957. Yes, oh yes, I was a painter; the new superintendent come in and they cut—the painting is off. They cut them out. In other words, if you had something to paint, they made me go paint. If there is nothing else—something don't get paint—they ought to go to the labor gang, any type of work. And I don't like that. See I was used to—my younger age with a brush in my hand. Now you give me pick and shovel. The body stiff, won't take it anyhow. So I ask him, I said, "You got anything better than this?" He say, "No." I say, "Well, how do you expect me to do this. I mean, I can't produce this labor job because I getting more older and I no used to this. Well, today my last day. That was in January. So I, I quit, and I left the job. I said the reason I ask him was I want to collect unemployment while I can't find nothing else.

Louis Glowaki makes deliveries, c. 1915-1920.

Louis and Marge Glowaki

The parents of both Louis and Marge Glowaki came from Poland before the turn of the century. Louis' father started a meat market business in 1892 and the business itself became a foundation for the family's entrance into banking, since a means had to be found for extending credit to customers. Marge's family entered a business pursuit of its own during the flu epidemic of 1918 in Plymouth.

LOUIS: Yes, my father started the [meat] business in 1891. Well years ago they used to go out country and slaughter them, you know. Buy it and slaughter at the place. My father had a lot of men working, you know, at that time. We had a couple—one or two men at that time. But in 1905, there was a strike. So my father closed up and he went to Europe for a vacation. When he come back, the strike was over. He opened up again. So he started the business again, so we have five teams going. We had a big business, a very big one; we had over twenty-two hundred customers. We butchered pigs every day. That's a lot of consumption, a lot of meats. To the doors, you know, we peddled door to door. Every team had a different route. Now I have a route—West Main Street, Normal Street, Church Street. The other fellow would have Union Street, Hanover Street, and thereon. The other fellow would go on eastside; he'd have Dover Street, Church Street, and Broad Street, and Dewey Park. And way back in 1913 I used to have a route on Eastwood Street all the way down to Lewis Park, Hanover Green and Parkwood Heights. We did our processing. We slaughtered and we processed.

MARGE: You used to go out to the country and buy the cattle and they used to slaughter them themselves.

LOUIS: Yes, we used to buy the cattle and have them hauled in by trucks. In those days we used to walk them in. And I tell you the truth, I walked from Nanticoke to Wapwallopen and then we cut two cows and walked back all the way to Nanticoke with two cows. Glowaki Meat Packing was the name of my father's business.

Q: Where was your father born?

LOUIS: In Europe. Poland. Lipnow. Very young man, I guess he was about seventeen years old then, seventeen or eighteen—1878, something like that. He came with one dollar. And I had that silver dollar, and my wife just misplaced it someplace and I don't even have it now. One dollar he had left when he landed in West Nanticoke. He was a young man and he was an orphan. His father was killed by a horse, runaway horse. And he was taken by relatives; he was raised by relatives. And he came here from Europe to Nanticoke when he's a young boy. I guess he was in his twenties. He landed in Nanticoke and he worked for his cousin, Joe Smith. That's his first job. Then he worked slaughtering cattle. That's a good many years ago, that's way back in 1888 or something like that. Then he went on his own. My mother died when she was twenty-seven. She came over to Schmidts, she was related to Schmidts. They had a butcher shop too. They were relatives. Sophie Chardinsky was my mother's name.

Q: Did your mother and father have a large family in Nanticoke, a lot of children?

LOUIS: Two girls and a boy, myself and my two sisters. My sisters graduated high school. She died but she graduated Oberlin University [College] in Ohio and I graduated Valparaiso University. I went to ninth grade and I went to Valparaiso University and I got my diploma for pharmacist. And at that time the war broke out. So I had to leave my father and go to the service. I was in service for year and a half; I come back to help my father. My father needed help so bad so I had to give up the druggist and enter the business. I took the business over. My father was still there, a figurehead, you know. He was helping me a lot, you know. But in 1917 I already started helping him. It got too big, you know; he couldn't handle it so I had to do all the work. I managed the business, I did the slaughtering, I did the buying and selling and everything else.

And I'll tell you, my father organized the Nanticoke National Bank. I'll tell you what happened. We had a big business and you know how $5 and $2, and $1 look stacked together? So he hand it over to the cashier. The cashier said, "John, why don't you put that money together in ones." He said, "That's what you get paid for." And my father got angry, took the money and he went uptown. Well, in a few weeks, he got friends like K. M. Schmidt to organize a bank. And he organized the Nanticoke National Bank. He says, you don't want my money, I took it out and went uptown. There was only one bank in Nanticoke, it was the First National at that time, and they were very independent, you know. They always dominated. So my father got mad. And he organized the bank. So today, I took his footsteps and I'm a vice-president of the bank.

Q: Let me ask you this, when the people working in the mines, I'm sure business was good, they could buy the meat. But what happened when they were out of work?

LOUIS: Well, I'll tell you, when my father died, I buried over a million dollars in credit. I made a bonfire out of it. Some people are very honest. I had money sent from Detroit, from Philadelphia, from Chicago. Some people were honest and their conscience bothered them and they sent me the money. But only five or six. Some were in Nanticoke and send me money after my father was dead. They were very honest people, but lots of them died and forgot. Well the people were working in the mines all the time. They had big families don't forget, five, six, seven, in the family. And I often wonder where the hell did they sleep. Five, six children in a four-room house. We had books. They took bills and marked them down in the book. We had an account of every customer. The depression didn't affect us at all. Not here, not in the mines, the miners were working steady that I know of. I didn't feel any depression. 'Course things were cheap. That's part of the reason why we existed because everything was cheap. And I bought a car for $15; today the same car would be worth about $250.

Q: Did the coal companies have much influence in the town? Did they— in the community, the area?

LOUIS: They had lots and lots of influence. They could boss over. They had to do it because it's either your job or you got to do what you're told. That's that.

Q: When you were a young man, did you have any ambitions, is there something you wanted to do? Let's say when you were fifteen, eighteen years old?

LOUIS: Well I was occupied with work, I never had no other thing but work, work, work. I used to get up 2:00 in the morning to go to country and looking for business all the time even on Sundays. Ask my wife, she'll tell you. There wasn't a Sunday that we didn't go out looking for cattle or something. Our Sundays were occupied, looking for business. That's all, that's all I had in mind. I had no pleasures.

MARGE: Keep the business going.

Q: When you were still in school, were you already working? Did you help out?

LOUIS: Oh yes. I was working then. Well, I started to work when I was fourteen years old. I went to the service for a year and a half, that's the only time I had off. I was in the service during the flu. I carried the bodies out almost twenty-four hours. I been near to a guy died, before you know it the other guy died, for twenty-four hours I had to stack the bodies up to the ceiling. And then when that kind of quieted down I was shipped to Philadelphia. And then in Philadelphia there was bodies in the back yard. You had no place to bury them. Then I come home, then I had a week's furlough. Then I come to Nanticoke: they were dying in Nanticoke. In Nanticoke they were dying too, but thank God I survived everything. In my crowd over there in Newport, Rhode Island, where I was stationed, we slept in groups you know. I was the only survivor of that group. I got up in the morning and I got busy, I didn't know what the hell happened. And first thing you know I went to sick bay and they took a physic and stayed out in that hot sun for three hours and that kind of cured me, I think.

Q: You mentioned that larger stores started to come in and hurt your business later on. . .when did that start to happen?

LOUIS: Well, that came away back in 1940, '45, '50. The business started to dwindle down you know. When the chain stores come in. By then you could treat it like you were out of business. I was in business till 1965. Then I quit because. . .first of all I couldn't make it go because stuff was too high, and besides. . .we didn't have much customers. They're all driving to the chain stores. So I had to give it up because I was over sixty-

31

five then. The new generation started it. The old generation was dying out and the new generation started going to the chain stores.

MARGE: And they started moving out.

LOUIS: Oh, like the late thirties to. . .the late fifties it started to dwindle down.

MARGE: Because they didn't want to work in the mines.

LOUIS: Young generation didn't want to work in the mines because they got this black lung you know, dust. The girls they were getting out too. The reason why the mines were busy, you see, because they had foreigners coming in; American boys don't want to work in the mines. They see. . .their fathers suffer from asthma, and that's an awful disease. It's a pity, it's a pity the way. . .you can't breathe, you can't breathe. You know that's the reason why a lot of boys don't even want to work in the mines.

MARGE: Some of them went to New Jersey, New York. They went to Baltimore, Detroit, all that young generation started going, you know. They got jobs down there.

LOUIS: Jobs, everything, they all went to work, lot of people work, New York, different categories. Lot of these girls are working in big hospitals. You see, the poorest families in all that had five or six children; three of those girls probably worked in New York, head nurses or something like that. I give them credit for that because they were born and brought up in a poor area and they made something out of themselves.

Q: When were the two of you married?

MARGE: In 1926. He was late for my wedding. And I called the priest up and he was coming into the church. We just had a simple wedding. At that time we didn't have hotels to go to, we'd have the weddings at home.
LOUIS: We just had a dinner and came to Atlantic City for a couple of days and come back quick.

Q: And what was your maiden name?

MARGE: Grontkowski. My father was an undertaker. In those days, at that time they didn't need a license, so he was an undertaker. Then all my brothers, my oldest brothers started becoming an undertaker and they had to be licensed. All my brothers became undertakers. In fact, in my family, we have thirteen undertakers. They followed the father's footsteps. Even their wives became undertakers. Two of my brothers were to-

32

gether in business. And after they got married, they separated. One started in Nanticoke and one started in Hazelton and one was in Plymouth. And my other brother became a monument dealer and he still is, just the other three are dead.

Q: As a young girl, did you work at all with them?

MARGE: Well, I only went to school to seventh grade because we had to quit at that time. At that time you didn't have to have—you weren't forced to go to school. So I left when I was in seventh grade. Well, then I stayed home and I got a job with the A&P and I worked for them for awhile, and then I got married and that was it.

Q: When you worked in the A&P did you contribute your wages to your parents?

MARGE: My mother was dead at the time, we each contribute our wages to the family that we'd have survive with us. My family also hauled coal.

LOUIS: The coal companies have a list of deliveries.

MARGE: They used to have horses for funerals. The wagons would deliver the miners to the home and from there they would notify the people. They would deliver them home by wagon. Then they would call the undertaker and have him take the body and embalm them and leave them in the house, and bury them. And there was a lot of competition in that time too because the undertakers were fighting for their business just like any other business. So the first one got there he's the one that got it. First one got to the home to notify the people. And that's how my brothers all started out. They're all very successful. Embalming was in the home. And then my brother, he was called into the service. And the flu broke out, he was taken out of the war and he was embalming for the service at that time because the people were dying. And they transferred him into Philadelphia and he worked for all of services. And the flu broke out there and after my other brother came home, the people started dying here, they couldn't get past this. So he was sent to bring caskets from Philadelphia into Plymouth in order to bury people. And they were so short of caskets that we have to have the lumber company make the caskets and we used to fix interiors. You know, put the blindings in, my sister and I. Most funerals were in the home. Open or half-casket, it all depended what the people wanted. My one brother, after he came back from the service, he was the first one to open up a funeral home. In Plymouth. He had a little chapel built, and then he started funerals in there. Because it made it more convenient for him. For this reason, that some people's homes were too small. And so he opened up this chapel and he used it.

Q: Could you briefly describe what they had to do when they went into a home?

MARGE: To a home and have to deliver the casket, the chairs, everything. It was for the people to have chairs to sit on. And they'd have the services from the home to the church. They used to take their equipment with them and embalm them. There were mine disasters, one in Avondale. And there's one here at Truesdale that my brother had thirteen of those people that were killed. About forty-six of them killed at that time in different areas. But from Plymouth there were sixteen and he had thirteen of those people to bury. And he had to bury them all.

Q: How would people react, I mean neighborhood-wise? Would people help out in periods of stress like this?

MARGE: Yes they did. People were very kind at that time. They were very helpful. Well, they would take food over for them, and they would sympathize with them. And they would stay there to help them out. They were very helpful, at that time. Today you don't have that. I think my father was on the border of Germany. My mother came from that area of Poland too. And she came over when she was sixteen. And never spoke English but she never left this country. And she's the one who started my brothers out; she used to go out and work. My father died when we were very young. And she worked very hard and she'd never let them go into the mines, so she worked very hard in order to start them out in business. We had a little farm that she worked to keep the food supply going, and after she got them started. They started to pick up more all the time and she didn't have to do it anymore. But then she died around 1926.

Kingston Coal Co. ambulance

Family and Community

George Treski and Stacia Treski

George Treski and Stacia Treski were both raised by parents who had emigrated from Poland in the 1890's. Ironically, both of their fathers had worked first in Pittsburgh mills before deciding to locate friends from their respective Polish villages who were then living in Nanticoke and obtaining employment in the mines. Reaching adolescence around 1930, George and Stacia knew full well how economic difficulties translated into family difficulties before and after their marriage. In this selection they relate the mechanics of family survival through the first half of their lives.

GEORGE: I grew up in Slocum Township on a farm with four brothers and four sisters. First, I started to work for the Lehigh and Wilkes-Barre Coal Company, but they closed down. I was only sixteen and my brother Stanley already worked there on consideration. That meant that you were not on piecework but worked for the company and got paid by the hour. Under consideration you might make as much as a contract miner who loaded a lot, but usually you made more than a laborer.

I went underground at age sixteen and the section foreman saw me and asked how old I was. I said, "Eighteen." He said, "You're a liar." But I stayed and gave my wages to my mother. I gave them to her until I was twenty-eight. I felt like turning it over and so did two of my brothers who still worked on the farm.

STACIA: When my father worked in the mines he decided to build another home himself even though they already had one. My parents figured that the extra home would get a little more income. They also thought that they had two children, so one home would eventually be for one girl and the other home for the second girl.

At that time, however, my father had an accident in the mines. The coal came down and knocked over a prop on my father's hand and took off four fingers. He could never go back to work anymore. And by 1931 he had black lung, although there was no compensation for that. He had black lung so bad he would only walk up the stairs once a day to go to bed.

I was going to school then and my sister was fourteen years old. She got a job in a silk mill where they paid ten cents an hour for ten hours a day, six days a week. So there was a little money. But after working one year she had a nervous breakdown and I had to put her in a mental hospital. I then went to look for a job. I was about fourteen or fifteen, and nobody in the family was working. This was around 1932, and you had to wait in long lines to find a job.

36

But we raised our own food, had our own chickens and ducks. We even tried to make moonshine. We sold a couple of quarts and got a little money that way. My mother was also the midwife for the area. She got paid in food—chickens, ducks.

We had three silk mills in town, a cigar factory and a sewing mill. Every morning you would make the rounds from one to another. You just stood there and maybe they would hire someone. If you knew someone maybe you got a job. The same as it is today. Maybe you had an aunt working there and they would talk to you.

I never did get a job, so I finished high school. That's the only reason I stayed in school. After I graduated I stayed at home over the summer and then in September I went to New York [City] to do housework for twenty-five dollars a month. The lady would even hold back five dollars a month to make sure you didn't quit.

A lot of girls from this area went to New York to work for Jewish families. One summer we even cleaned houses at the ocean. And my parents wanted fifteen dollars a month from me, so what could I buy myself? They wanted it every month when you came home. When we were in New York we didn't do much except visit free museums, eat hot dogs, and drink orange juice.

When I was a teenager I always wanted to be a nurse. But how could you get to be a nurse? I mean you just couldn't. If you didn't have money you just didn't go to school. We really didn't have any money. My father wasn't working; my sister had a nervous breakdown. We finally went on relief. Everybody needed it. My parents didn't realize though that when they took it you had to have a lien on your house. First they gave us $7.50 a week, but then an investigator would come along and practically tell you how to live. And if you had anyone staying in the house like a married daughter or a married son you had to hide them when the investigator came along because they would want to know if there was any extra money coming in. In fact, when my father died my mother had an insurance policy, and we had to pad all the expenses of his funeral, like a new suit. We didn't really buy him a suit. We went to a place where they sell suits and had them give us a bill. We needed to keep a little bit of that money from the insurance.

We never did lose our home. After I married I lived there with my mother. My husband was going to a school to be a mechanic. Even when he was going to school I went back to New York and did some more housework.

My sister then returned from the State hospital and we took her in. She always had illusions that someone was chasing her, but someone had to care for her.

I'll tell you that when we were small we didn't get a lot of good food to eat. If you got sick and had a fever they gave you oranges because they thought they had to. I was so darn skinny all the years I went to school I had "malnutrition" on my card. The people at school who examined you would stamp your card. They would look at you and say you had malnutrition and that your mother should take you to the doctor. He would say you needed milk. Well, my mother would go out and buy one quart of milk and that's the last quart of milk you would see for months. We had chickens and ducks but never any red meat. And we only had vegetables in the summer. We got some fruit from the hucksters that would come around. It was the same old diet all the time with chicken soup on Sunday and cabbage and potatoes. Everyone had a cabbage barrel and lots of potato pancakes.

GEORGE: By the early 1930's you was only getting a few days [of work] a week. Usually your pay would run out pretty fast. You'd only get two or three days' pay for two weeks.

We would then work on the family farm to get more food. You had to depend on the farm to get food. We would kill hogs, calves. You raised your own potatoes and cabbage. So we at least had food.

This was still my parents' farm. I stayed there until I was twenty-eight and got married.

STACIA: There really wasn't any money. During a strike in 1935* there was a young man that went to work and his wife was expecting a baby. He was from this area and had to work because he had two children and a wife who was expecting another. He went to work—crossing the pickets—and was killed in an accident in the mines. The people were so mad that he went to work they wanted to dig him out. They had to get the police to keep him in his grave. But the strikers didn't like the idea that he went to work.

There was another man who went to work and not only the men got after him but the women got after him too. They stripped him of his clothes and he had to go home without any clothes on. Because he worked and they called him a scab. Everyone else's husband was sitting at home and he went to work.

After marriage my husband wasn't working steady so he went to Patterson, New Jersey. I stayed here, but I didn't like the idea. He had a sister in Patterson so I moved out there and we had a baby. We lived in New Jersey for four years; this was during the war [1941-1945]. But the first

---

*This was the strike of insurgent mine workers in the anthracite area against the United Mine Workers.

An anthracite wedding

Henry Molski, Glen Lyon

day the war was over the factory closed down. There was no more job. We were in New Jersey for four years and saved five thousand dollars, so when we came back to Nanticoke we bought a tire business and lived with my mother again. We had two children by now. But my husband was so soft-hearted he would fix tires for his friends, do them favors, and never charge them. Sometimes we didn't have money for milk. So George went into the mines for two more years. But he would come home so wet, so black, coughing, and everything, we looked for something else [he could do] with machines.

Irene Wieczorek

Irene Wieczorek was born in 1923 in Nanticoke. Like many women growing up in mining families, she was tied strongly to family obligations throughout her life. She tells of her family ties and especially the care she rendered to her mother.

WIECZOREK: Well as far as I know my father was born in Pennsylvania, in Nanticoke. It was Nanticoke to be exact. And Mom was born here. Now Mom's parents were married here but Pop's came from the old country. Where exactly in Poland I don't know. Mom and Pop settled in Nanticoke. Mom was from Warrior Run and there were eight children and two died. One was two and a half and one was four and a half. And the six of us were living until November 5, 1977; my sister just passed away. As far as that we weren't strict Polish but we were to the sense that we were Polish and we all attended parochial school. There was a school in West Nanticoke that I remember. My father went as far as fifth and sixth grade, and then I think, when he was eleven or twelve, he started picking up slate around the mines and that. You know that happen. And Mom started in the cigar mill. Mom went up to the eighth grade; she was educated considering those days, you know. And then she started in the cigar mill. I think she was only twelve or thirteen at the time.

Q: Did your father always work in the mines?

WIECZOREK: Yes, all his life. He died at fifty-one or fifty-two, with asthma. Yes, when he was younger he worked around the mines and when he was old enough to go into the mines, he used to go into the mines. You know nine years old. They used to be carrying their buckets; men would help them carry their buckets and everything. At that time women didn't work like they do now. The man thought that the woman's place was at home I guess. And she had the eight children really. She had her hands full, believe me; she had eight children in twelve years.

Q: You mentioned that your grandparents had come over here from Poland. Did they ever say to your parents why they came to this particular area?

WIECZOREK: Well it was always somebody came before them, you know, and they found they like the section. So then when they wrote home, they saved the money and then they came. I think Grandma and Grandpa came with only Aunt Francie and then she had eleven children or something, and some died and she only had six left afterwards, but then she had the others here in America. I had only one brother living. The oldest sister graduated and the next one didn't want to go to school, so she quit when she was sixteen; I graduated; Teresa didn't want to go to school. After high school we had to more or less go out looking for work, because it was hard, it was really hard. So I started—I don't know if you would remember, they had the NYA (National Youth Administration) a long time ago. You worked so many hours a week or a month and then you got, I think it was $26.50. It was more or less part-time to help the poor people get on their feet. So in the meantime the war came up, and I went to Maryland. We lived in Oxford, Pennsylvania and we commuted every day. Me and my sister. I worked there ten months and Mom got sick so one of us had to come home. So I was younger, I had to come home. So then when Mom came home from the hospital I worked in Dupont. So I worked there until it closed, nine and a half years about. So then I went to Kingston a little bit, but it was on the all-night and it was traveling and I got car sick. We went in a car. Like a group of us when the plant closed. We went together, there were six of us. And then afterwards I was home and the McGregor's moved into town over here on Washington Street, so I went there and I worked there for seventeen and a half years. So they moved to Berwick and I took a layoff because Mom was in Valley Crest a few years and I came home to take care of her. So then I took a layoff and I was collecting security and I took care of Mom and then after my security ran out, I got a job in Pitt Fuller; it was a shoe factory, and I worked on baby shoes there. Our wages went into the household really, because when I got to working, and that, it was helping the other children to go to school. And it gave them a few little luxuries. When I got older, Mom used to take only half of the pay, because she could see her way like to take care of the house as is. My mother handled the money. Pop never wanted to handle it; he said he couldn't make it last as far as Mom did. My mother was a wizzard with money, believe me, because she didn't get that much at the time; so after us kids got to work it was easier for them. The pity part I always say and I always will say, when Pop could enjoy his life, he had to leave us. We were all working and he could have lived good; he wouldn't have to worry about working even though he wasn't feeling good. But the asthma really got so bad that he died from that.

Q: How about your sisters and brother did they turn their paychecks over to them?

WIECZOREK: Yes, it was just a family standard with us. I mean nobody had any qualms about it. We did it ourself. Mom always would give us every pay an allowance and with that we would buy our powder and stuff like that and go to dances. My Mom always liked us to go out; you know she didn't want us to bum around. But yet she liked us to go to dances, to the movies and things like that.

41

When I first started in McGregor's—like this union, they really helped me out, because it was the way they did things in McGregor's. When they first came here, they'd hire so many people. You would work a couple of months and they would lay you off. When it came time for a raise they'd lay you off and hire new people. So it was on the day I was laid off that the union had a meeting and it was just about two weeks before I was supposed to enter the union and the girl said to me, "Come on to the union meeting, maybe they can do something for you." So we went to the union meeting, there was four or five of us girls together and we spoke to the union man about it. So that's when he got McGregor's on the carpet about that. See it was the procedure they followed all the time. Instead of paying the rates, because every so often you were eligible for a raise, they used to lay you off and hire new people. So that's where the union helped me. So really they have their good points and they have their bad points.

We moved quite a bit because the children [were growing and] my Mom always had to be moving into a bigger home you know. I would say we lived in mixed neighborhoods. The first landlady was Lithuanian; she spoke her language and we spoke ours and we each understood each other. Of course I don't understand Lithuanian too much, but Mom understood. But the majority of the people can understand Polish regardless of what nationality they are. And then we lived next door to Italians and I mean we all got along well. But before I think neighbors were nicer to live with, than what it is today.

Q: You mention your one sister quit school. How did your parents feel about that?

WIECZOREK: Well Mom didn't like it, and Pop was sort of neutral, because the only time he took a hand was when we really needed it, a little bit heavy-handed, you know. He never hit us, but he hollered and we were scared. But Mom didn't think she wanted her to quit school because, under the circumstances, they felt if you had more education you could get a better job and that was the way that went. But since she was sort of stubborn about it, so her marks weren't too good and she sort of just didn't want to go to school, so she ended up in the General Cigar Mill. And she worked there quite a few years. That was the only stipulation that she could quit school, was to go to work. Mom said if you quit school, you will have to get a job, you know. That was more or less to discourage her from quitting school. Now the other sister that quit school, she worked two years and then she wanted to go back to school, but see she was already nineteen at the time. And Mom says, "If you couldn't see your way to go at sixteen or seventeen, you're too old now."

So that was it. She said you wanted to work, so work, get married and go to school and that was it.

Q: What did your parents want you to do? What did they see for you?

WIECZOREK: Well like she [mother] wanted me to go to training as a nurse and of course, they always wanted everybody to get married good. In other words, not that you had to marry rich but she wanted you to have a good husband and a good life. The oldest married a Swedish boy, and Betty married a Polish, and now I am going with a Russian. Teresa married a Dutch and Timmy married a Russian girl and Sylvie married a Polish. So we always say we are a league of nations. Mother never really like voiced an opinion like some mothers would push their children. She always felt that we would always do what we wanted to do, and the only thing she did stress was living a good life.

Q: What age or how old were you when you started doing household chores?

WIECZOREK: Oh heavens. As early as you could walk and understand, believe me. There was always a chart, because we all had our little chores to do. Even now I can remember when I was in high school, I broke my leg and in those days you didn't go to the hospital and lay for six weeks, you stayed home. I had crutches and the table was on one side and the sink was on the other side, so they used to put a chair in the middle and I would sit down and one would wash and I would dry the dishes and put them on the table, and that's the chart. Everybody had a job to do. So it was always you did this, and this one did that, and that one did that. Mom used to always have little jobs for all of us. She always felt busy fingers didn't get in trouble. We helped. One peeled carrots, one peeled potatoes, one did the onions. Now baking too, Mom was a good baker and we always helped around the kitchen. My brother always had what we called the boy's work to do. Pop used to always delegate jobs for him, but Mom like Timmy more of less, so she would say, "Irene you help brother with this." This one do this and that one that and brother wanted to go out in the field and play baseball.

If going to church and that is very religious, Mom and Pop was religious as far as that goes, but they were not what you would call fanatics. We used to always talk, when we went to church. We would always take up the whole seat, because it was Mom and all the kids sharing. When there was little ones Mom would take all the little kids and Pop would stay home with the baby and then he would go to another mass. Now vesper and different special occasions, Pop didn't go too much because he was more or less too tired, but we always went, the children. But in the

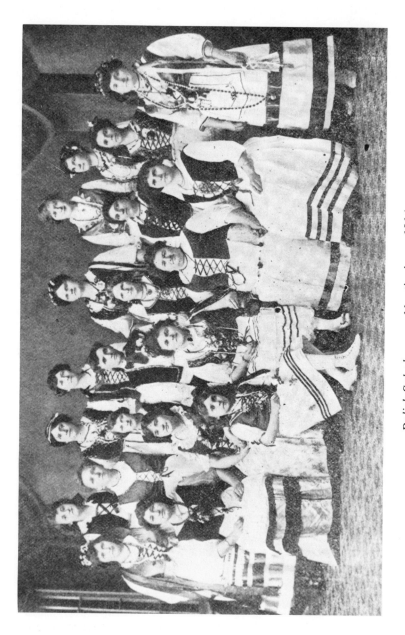

Polish Sokol group, Nanticoke, c. 1914

sense that Mom used to force us, no. She would always ask if we wanted to go and if we felt like going and that. I would always say that they were more American than strictly old-fashion Polish. Now in those days, like there were Jewish people and stuff like that, like some Polish people they wouldn't allow their kids to go with the English and stuff like that. Now Mom was never like that; I went to school with English and a Welsh and whoever was in the neighborhood, and Italian and that, and Mom never stressed friends only that they had to have a good reputation. If she felt that somebody wasn't living right, she didn't want us to more or less go with them, but she always felt that we should learn at a young age to try and pick our friends ourself, and so, sometimes you pick good, sometimes you pick bad. You learn who's good and who's bad and who takes advantage of you. I'm the oldest and still get taken advantage of.

Marie Skovranski

Because mining families generally struggled to make ends meet, children raised in such families often felt a deep sense of responsibility to assist their parents by beginning work as soon as possible. Marie Skovranski grew up in just such a family and reveals how she left school to help her mother.

SKOVRANSKI: My father's people came from Poland; this is where they settled [Nanticoke]. And my dad was born and raised here, and that's why after my mother passed away they wanted me to sell the property. And I couldn't do it because I could see my father building these two places here all by himself after work. I just couldn't give it up—there is too many memories here. My father's family all went to work because their dad died when he was forty-two, and my grandmother was left with twelve children. And there was no relief. There was no help of any kind at that time, so she went out on the farms to work and all the girls as soon as they were old enough, as soon as they were ten or eleven years they were working; they had to. My grandma went out to work and they went to a silk mill. My mother was born in West Nanticoke. This is where she raised most of her family. But my mother told me they had it very hard and my dad always liked my mother. My dad came from a wealthier family and she always said that I was too poor for you. My dad would say that he didn't look for wealthy, I want you for my wife, and that's the way it's going to be. See my dad went to a wedding—one of his friends was getting married and of course my mother couldn't afford a gown or anything, so she didn't go to this wedding. So she stood out and watched. You know how in the olden days they used to stand around and watch weddings. My dad came out to talk to her and that's how they got acquainted. And he ask her out to dinner that night and she looked at him and she thought, I don't even have any clothes to go out with him. And he said, I'm not looking for your clothes, I just want to go out with you. And from then on they started dating and he was determined to get married.

My father always worked in the mines. There was something about the mines, now, I don't know what it was, and yet he would do all this work when he came home from the mines, and if he didn't he would take the books out and study, because they didn't get the opportunity like the kids today have going to school. At the time when I was in eighth grade, my brother took sick and my mother, and of course, I was going to parochial school at the time, and my mother ask me to take time off to give her a hand out at home, which I did. And after my brother passed away she ask me to go back to school. And I said, "Mother, I was too far back with my studies," which disappointed my parents very much. My dad gave me violin lessons and my sister. So in them days there was no buses—you had to walk—and then it was scary—we had to go home after school because we went down on Bartfield Street—where we had a school. And after school we had to go and there was no lights, no taxis and no buses—we had to walk home. I came home one night and I said, "Father, I think I am going to quit." He said, "Why?" I was doing good in school and I said, "Dad, I'm afraid, and it's awfully dark and I'm the only student from Honeypot." I was the only student from Honeypot then. My sister just made up her mind she didn't want to go. My dad had plans and we just failed him, that was it.

We learned some Polish. In fact, I can write in Polish. When we went to receive Holy Communion you know you had to go school, in them days four years before you can receive, and of course my mom wanted to send us to the Irish school. My dad said, "No, we were going to the Polish school because that's what they are, they're Polish and that's where they are going." I was never sorry a day in my life. I read and write and I do everything, I can sing in Polish, and I was so proud because I can even write letters as far as that goes. I never did regret that. I have neighbors that have changed their name; I would never do that. I'm not ashamed of my background. I can't see why they would do it. Well I know when I just got married, my husband's name was very complicated to spell, and every place I had to spell the name. So then I started to give my name short like his sister in Pittsburgh, and he got mad at me. He said, "Now look, that is not the right thing to do. That wouldn't be right." And I thought, well I didn't want to go to court because I thought that was silly to go through and change my name and all, so I kept it up.

Q: What did you do after you quit school?

SKOVRANSKI: No, I didn't do anything. I stayed home and helped my mother, because my mother was a dressmaker. She used to make wedding gowns and everything, she used to do a lot of sewing. But see she had a shop of her own, here behind the house she had a shop. She had a lot of customers.

Chester Brozena

Chester Brozena was born in Plymouth in 1908 and started working as a young man in a coal breaker. He provides excellent accounts of the activities of the United Anthracite Miners and the disgust of the rank and file with the United Mine Workers. He also offers a view into the network of mutual assistance which sustained the mining communities through both emotional and economic difficulties.

Q: Who did your grandfather work for?

BROZENA: The Lehigh and Wilkes-Barre Coal Company. Yeah that was it. They had the Lance breaker, they had the Nottingham breaker, they had the Number 12 and the Washington. At that time, jobs were plentiful. You could quit one job in the morning and start somewhere in the afternoon, you know—night shift. Jobs were plentiful during that time. Maybe conditions got so as that you couldn't stand them—you didn't like the boss or any number of reasons. Maybe the pay was better somewhere else, or the work was easier, or you had a friend say, "Come down, I'll get you a job where I'm working." It all tied in. His main occupation was the assistant manager in a grocery store, a small chain grocery store in town. But then the pay—with a bunch of children, seven children, the pay was so small he had to get out and get in the mines where the money was much better.

As a child, it was circumstances. If your father said, if you want to continue on school you can; but then all your buddies went to work. They were going uptown with a dollar in their pocket and you didn't have any, so you said, "Well, the hell with this, I'm going to get a job," and you did. So at fourteen years old you went and got your working papers and got a job. I worked in a coal breaker to begin with, in the Kingston Coal Company. From there on, I went to Avondale, and Lee. Our tenant in our house was a foreman up there, assistant foreman. He got me the job.

Q: What did you do as a breaker boy?

BROZENA: Well, there were slate pickers, but he didn't start me that way. There were different occupations. There was shakers up where they dump the cars. Then there was the chute, where it would separate the

47

sizes of coal. Then there was what they call the higs, where the rock would be separated—a lot of the rock, but not all. Then the breaker boys were the last ones that would pick out the pieces of slag and rock or slate or whatever. I started out mostly as a shaker changer, a little better job than a slate picker. You brought your pay home, and then your mother gave you whatever, fifty cents or seventy-five cents. Of course it cost a nickel to go to the movies, a nickel for a bag of candy, or so on. So expenses wasn't that great, unless you started smoking or chewing tobacco or something. Then of course you needed a little more spending money. But on the whole, you turned your pay in up to your parents.

I stayed there maybe two years or so. Then I went to Avondale. There was a neighbor of ours was foreman at Avondale, and he got me a job outside which paid more money as outside labor.

During strikes in 1925 we went up and found a coal hole, and carried coal out, and sold it to people. This is how you sustained yourself.

Q: What do you mean, you found a coal hole?

BROZENA: You went up in the mountain, and dug a hole, and found coal up there. Then you carried it out, cracked it, and then you sold it to business people along Main Street, because there was no other source of coal. So you sold them the coal, and that's the way you [lived]. There was no Welfare, and there was no food stamps; there was no benefits of any kind. The fellow in the region—if there ever was a monument built, it should be [to] the small storekeeper. He was the guy that kept you on the book. Otherwise, you'd never won a strike here. When you went to the store, you bought what you called on the book. You got your pay every two weeks, then you went and you paid. When a strike came, why, he just kept on taking on his book, and you didn't pay him until you started back to work. But if he had demanded his money when it was due, then you couldn't have survived. So he is the real hero of the coal mines, the storekeeper, the individual storekeeper. Well, you done whatever you could to help the family. Like say the neighbor died here [the neighbor here died]. The first thing, my wife would go and get a ham or some kielbasa or so on, and send it up. If there was small children, you'd help take care of the smaller children. Everybody helped. It's getting away from that somewhat today because when there was a funeral before, you'd have twenty, twenty-five cars. Everybody'd take a day off around the family. Today even the family don't take a day off. You see one car in a funeral procession, where years ago the whole family took the time off. And they buried them from the house, which was charitable. They was three days and three nights that nobody slept, ate or washed, or anything else because the house was full of people. But now they go to the funeral parlor, and that's all over with.

48

Homes of miners and families

I was president of Avondale union, but we started a new union at that time [1934]. I went [to] the union meeting and asked about getting some aid. We had then eight, nine children, were working two, three days a week. So I asked if we couldn't get some aid from the district office. The president of the union at that time, district president, was John Boylan. His salary was $15,000 a year, at that time. So, I went to the meeting, and asked if some of the members couldn't get aid. In the meantime, someone had dynamited Boylan's home. So when our representatives from our local went to the convention or whatever, semi-convention, they came back with a report that they couldn't get any aid for the members; but they voted to pay for repairing Boylan's home and offer so much reward for the capture of the dynamiters. This really threw everybody in an uproar and they said, "The hell with them." So there was a convention called by a fellow by the name of Thomas Maloney and Rinaldo Cappellini—one-armed fellow. He was a very fiery Italian union leader here. He called a convention and we thought it was just sort of to try and straighten our outfit out, but instead of that they went off to a new direction. They went to what they called a new union. That was in 1934 and that's when all the turmoil was. Not under United Mine Workers, I didn't—under the new union, I was elected.

Q: If a man was a head of a local, would he tend to get a better job in the mines?

BROZENA: Lots of times, yes. If he was helping call the company work, like go along and fix track, and he'd put up props or timber where it was needed. But, there was no set amount of work he had to do, so if he didn't feel good that day, he could go in and sleep all day, and nobody bothered him.

Q: And he'd still be paid?

BROZENA: And he'd still be paid, sure. You was paid so much an hour a day, and your pay was assured. It wasn't like the contract miner, who had to get his cars and load them to get paid. Company work, you was assured your pay; it was like six, seven dollars a day, whatever. You was assured that, regardless of what you did or what you didn't do.

Q: Why then did you become particulary dissatisfied with the local officials?

BROZENA: Well, we were only working a couple days a week, and as you start going to the meetings, you got interested in it, because you listened to the radio and Avondale's working today. Then Avondale and Nottingham is working tomorrow, and it was one, two, three days a week. They were trying to give everybody some little time. You start going to union meetings, and wondering what the district was going to do for members that needed help, and then they come back and told you nothing. So then that's when everybody started throwing chairs around and got in an uproar, and says no way we're paying dues the same as soft coal. We were assessed three dollars a month for a long period of time to help soft coal because they were down on their knees, and when we tried to get some help from soft coal, we were turned down by John L. Lewis. That was another reason. He never even came in during our problems here, and he built something like eleven hospitals in the soft coal, and their pension rights are great and so on, and they never came to the hard coal rescue. That was the purpose of Anthracite Miners, to break away from John L. Lewis and his United Mine Workers because he was strictly soft coal.

Q: Why do you think that was so? Why do you think Lewis was neglecting anthracite?

BROZENA: Well, all the money was in soft coal, I guess, so this didn't bother him because at that time there were about 175,000 men in the anthracite in the three districts. I think that was district one, seven and nine. The worst evil that happened around the mines was the checkoff. Before that, they'd have a button committee standing at the mine gate, at the mine entrance. And they would collect your dues there. Then the officials sort of had to be on the ball a little bit, because you'd kind of hold

50

back your dues, or you wouldn't pay them. When the checkoff came, all he had to do was keep his feet on the desk and the money rolled in. So nobody had to care what they done for you or what they didn't do. You had to pay your dues, and it was closed shop—you couldn't work without belonging to the union. There was no choice for you. You had to go along and whatever they do. So this is why everybody got sick of John L. Lewis, because he never came in to see what our problems was, why we couldn't have better conditions, or why we couldn't get a little help. At Avondale we elected a slate for the new union. Officers retained their status in the United Mine Workers. We had a good local, we had about four hundred members in that mine Avondale, and we had about 390 that belonged to the new union, so we were pretty strong. Even though they didn't recognize it, they knew that if we said there's no work, they knew there wouldn't be no work. See, some were pretty well split. So the foreman was playing one against the other and he was having a ball, but our foreman had no choice. When you said, don't take no lamps out, nobody took no lamps. For instance, a man by the name of Johnny O'Toskey loading the car and a chunk of rock was on the top. The foreman's name was Frank Mayday, and the superintendent was Sandy Henderson. And they fired him. They fired this guy because of loading rock. He wasn't supposed to put this load of rock on. Anyhow we went down and tried to plead for him [O'Toskey] to give him his job back, and they wouldn't listen. So next morning we went down to the lamp room and everybody came and took out their lamps. So when they came there, the bosses came in and just told everybody coming down, don't take a lamp; so everybody stood along by the way there along the highway lamp shanty. "What are you going to do?" "Johnny goes to work, we go to work. Johnny don't go to work, we don't." So we hung around about five to seven and finally said, "All right, go ahead." And that's how we won is we had control of it. In other places it was sort of fifty-fifty, and it was harder.

Q: Why at Avondale are you more successful?

BROZENA: Well they got kind of disillusioned with the leadership in our particular local [UMW]. They were good fellows and all, but they were just taking care of themselves more than they were the people. We made little incentives. If your dues were paid up, and you got hurt, you got a dollar a day while you was hurt, and so on. We put in little things that made it more attractive for people to join our cause. We thought then we'd deal directly with our own instead of whatever John L. Lewis done down there we had to abide by. This way, we could eliminate him and we had enough—175,000 people—that we could carry on our own business here. Yeah, well, like I say, Boylan was a [UMW] district leader at that time, had done nothing. When Boylan's home was dynamited and the union offered a reward to pay for the capture of the dynamiters plus repair of his home after his getting $15,000 salary, our members couldn't even get a bag of flour. Like I say, breaking away from John L. Lewis. It came about in a funny way. Anthracite Miners—Tom Maloney, Cappelini, and those fellows—they were holding a convention line, a rump convention at Scranton. So I was elected as a delegate from our local to attend this rump convention. At this rump convention was where the change came about. Instead of going along with trying to improve conditions in the United Mine Workers, they—Cappelini and them—decided we'd go along with a new union. So you came back and made a report to the membership and they decided to go along with Cappelini. Everything was in order, it was just a matter of everybody had enough of John L. Lewis at that time.

Lance was a good colliery. That was number eleven. Nottingham. This side of the river was fairly good, but it wasn't too bad. Woodward was with Scally Edmunds, was a good leader up there. He was a good leader. Some of these were easier because in the Woodward and some of these collieries there was factions within the United Mine Workers, so it wasn't too hard to take over. If you belonged to one faction, then they'd follow you into the other groups. There had been always dissension and dissatisfaction among the locals. When elections came, there was always factions that ran. So this is what happened. Down in Glen Lyon they seemed, I think, they had better conditions than we did—the Susquehanna Coal Company and so on. And I think they worked steadier and had better conditions and this is where they didn't follow through as much as we did, because our conditions were terrible. One day a week, two days a week, and so on. Fifteen dollars I work, I was getting seventy-two cents an hour, we worked ten hours a day. Well $7.20 at that time was good money, but you only worked two days in two weeks, so you came home $15.40 in two weeks. Like I say you either picked coal or lived in my father's house. There the rent was low. If you didn't have it, you didn't pay it, and this was it. The storekeeper was the guy—because you owed him thirty, you went in and give him ten, and he accepted it. This is how you managed to survive.

In 1935 there was twenty-nine of us from the United Anthracite Miners called into court in Wilkes-Barre by Judge Valentine. Our people rallied around us, they came to the courthouse that day, but there was two hundred State policemen came out from behind the courthouse with clubs—they just battered everybody out of the way and chased everybody out. We were called up and got in front of Judge Valentine and he demanded that we call off the strike. We were on strike. They said they can't call it off—I didn't call the strike, the members called it. So we were all sent to jail on contempt of court. We spent thirty-two days in jail. Oh yeah, murderer's row. That was the time Bobby Edwards—that was before your time—when he had killed a girl out at Harvey's Lake and they put us in this murderer's row. They fingerprinted us, took our pictures, just like regular criminals, and we're only in there for contempt of court. There was some people that was interested, and they tried to get the Civil Liberties Union* interested, but I guess somehow along the line it got lost. But then after that, we kept going downhill because people started going back to work, because how long could they stay out? Finally Tommy Miller, the Pennsylvania Railroad attorney—he became congressman one term—got us together—Bill Moore and Red Peters, Stanley Edmunds and sons—so he took us down to Glen Alden Coal Company office. Billy Engles was there—he was president of the coal company—and some other officials, I don't remember. Anyway, it was a question that we just had to give up because the courts was against us, United Mine Workers were against us. We told them that we admitted that the thing was over, that we couldn't go any further. There was only one concession you asked for, and that was to let our people go back to work, not penalize them for being out. That was trying to lead on. So then we came down to Nottingham Colliery yards. We had a mass meeting and of course some of them didn't want to give in—Red Peters and them stood up and said we'll fight. Then I told them to get up and I said go back to work. I said this is the agreement we made, so do you want your job back? Go back to work. This is over. And it was over. Well, you know how it is, you got die-hards. But what was the use of carrying on when you was only hurting yourself? You wasn't going to get anywhere. There was no way you were going to get anywhere. Just people, but what they said, so you had a couple dollars and you used that up, so what was you going to do? You had to go back. So these people were sneaking back, your best friends were going back, your own family members were going back, so what was the use of holding out? I had an uncle—he's dead now—but he stuck right in. The fellow that owned the house here, he stuck right to the last minute, he didn't give in. And others, a number of them. My uncle and aunt and different ones, but there was one or two of the family that did go back to work. But then after you forgot it all—what was the use of carrying on something that was dead. Yeah. Well, it was a fact, that was all. The only thing is, you tried to save your members. Save their jobs, that was all, so they wouldn't [suffer] reprisals, you know.

Well I didn't go back into the mines. I just had enough of it. So then in

*The American Civil Liberties Union did investigate the case and concluded that officials of the Glen Alden Coal Company and local political officials had infringed upon the men's civil rights.

'37 I got a job in the courthouse up to '41 and then '41 we lost the election. Then the war started, so I went down to New Jersey and got a job. I then came back in '46 or '47 and built a gas station in Plymouth with a partner, then sold out to the partner and went to work for Kingston Mining Company. That was Morgan Burr's outfit. Worked there till 1952, then went back down to New Jersey.

Q: Did most of those twenty-nine men get back into the mines? Did they want to?

BROZENA: Most of them, yeah. Well we had a lot of sympathy in the beginning, because people knew what the situation was, because you had pay envelopes that—not one penny in them, after two weeks' work. And there was so much free work that had to be done, putting your own room in, and crops in. You weren't getting paid for that, no. Lots of times you went home with four cars instead of six cars a shift, and that's all it paid. They had to buy their own powder, their own dynamite; they had to pay for that, the blasting caps, pay their labor. You had to pay a nickel a day for the lamp on your head. After a while it got to where it wasn't profitable to mine. Scavengers took over mining. The usual procedure to mine was to go to the line—they called it—robbing back. You drove in. Then you started what they called robbing and you kept robbing—caving—behind it. Well, then these fellows get in and they robbed going in. Wherever they could get a car of coal, this is what they did. And this is how they got it.

Q: Some people have said that a lot of other industries tried to come in here throughout the years, but the coal companies prevented them.

BROZENA: They did, yes. Oh yes. I couldn't name them offhand, but corporations wanted to come here. You see, what their aim was—and they were very effective—they wanted a surplus of labor because every day you'd go [to] any colliery entrance, their office, and you'd see ten, twelve guys standing around looking for work. So when there was something that the boss would tell you to do in the mines, and you told him that you wasn't going to do it, well, then, he said, if you don't want to do it there's fifteen guys outside waiting for your job. This was their song all the time. So what did you do? You either did it or you lost your job. They wanted a surplus all the time. They had it, too.

Q: And they owned most of the land, didn't they?

BROZENA: Oh yeah. Everything between them and say the Scranton Spring Water Company and so on. I don't think they ever bought it or anything. The same as mineral rights. You're sitting on coal and they can come down and take it right out from under you.

The Miners

Labor gang, Glen Lyon breaker, 1930's

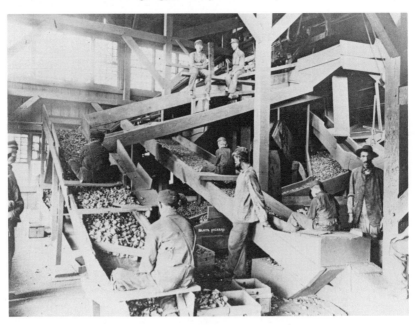

Slate pickers

Joe Sudol, John Sarnoski
and Romaine Stewart

In the anthracite mines of Pennsylvania men continually confronted the power of not only mine operators but officials of the United Mine Workers. Reactions of rank and file miners to the various forms of authority they faced and the demands of the workplace are delineated clearly by the three men in this interview. Joe Sudol, born in 1905 to immigrant parents from Poland, entered mining like his father and brothers and eventually found his way to the mining community of Glen Lyon. John Sarnoski came to America at age nineteen and secured a job laboring for his brother-in-law who was a contract miner. Romaine Stewart, born in 1912 to a Dutch father and Scotch-Irish mother, entered a breaker at Wanamie at age sixteen. These men all worked unknowingly toward a common future in the Glen Lyon-Wanamie area. They vividly recall the limits of worker power.

SUDOL: My father had five sons and I was the second oldest. We all had to go to work in the breaker picking slate. Well, there was rock and coal coming down the chute. You had to pick the rock from the coal. There would be a fellow who would let so much coal come down in this section and then send it to another section where a group of boys would keep picking.

There was a breaker boss and assistant foreman. They would watch you. If you let some rock go through he would poke you in the back with a stick and tell you what you missed. "Get it all out." Up on top someone would pick and cut big rocks before it went into the rollers. My older brother Adam was already in the breaker. After the breaker we both went to the mines to be "nippers," that is spragging cars. You put a stick of wood in the wheels to stop cars of coal coming from the mines. You couldn't let cars fall back down a grade into the mines. It would knock the timber down and you would have a mess. After three or four years of being a nipper you would become a motorman. Well, the motorman would supply the empty cars back to the miners to load again. But you had to work at least five years there as a laborer before you would become a miner. I labored longer than that though.

When the West End [Coal Co.] gave out I came to Glen Lyon and that's where I became a miner. I was doing mostly motorman work in Mocanaqua, but then when I came to Glen Lyon I landed a job laboring for a while before I became a miner.

It was not hard to get a job in either place. There was always an opening for work because they were always digging more openings. If one area caved in they would start a hole in a different section. Here in Glen Lyon they were digging into at least six different veins. We never took out the coal that was hard to get, only what we could get the easiest.

When I was a youngster, a union organizer met my dad in Mocanaqua and asked him to go to West Virginia to organize the union down there. The organizer felt the best way to organize a union was to get a job and work in the mine so you could talk with the men. So he took my dad with him. We first moved into Glen White, West Virginia, then we moved to McAlpin and then to Eccles and finally to Tams. At Tams the superintendent was the mine foreman and everything. He told my father to load his furniture and move out because he didn't want no union in there. My dad said we'll organize the union whether you like it or not. So he went over the hill to Eccles and organized the union over there.

In Glen White the superintendent didn't want my father to leave though because he knew his timber work. That's what they liked. When he put up a set of timber it was done right.

My father understood four languages and spoke Polish. That's the real reason they wanted him to work as an organizer. He understood, Polish, Slavish [Slovak], Hungarian and English. And there were a lot of Hungarians down there. When he spoke to the men he was welcomed in the homes.

He came to Pennsylvania because he didn't like working in soft coal. He felt there was more dust and [therefore] more explosions. We lived in one town and there was an explosion in the next one. I remembered walking over the hill and saw all those people who were killed were laid out. What a smell from the explosion that burned them people. My father seen that and he figured, "This is not for me. I'm going back to hard coal."

I then went into West End Coal Company and every one of my brothers followed me. Frank, George and Mike came after me. Adam later left the mines and landed a job in a foundry in Berwick. My younger brothers went into trades. One became a cabinetmaker and another a plumber. My father was a carpenter before he came to America. Same with me. Before I came to Glen Lyon I was a carpenter around the mines. My father taught us carpentry. Even my grandfather was a carpenter near the Russian border. But my father never forced me to go into the mines. I wanted to go. It was better than picking potatoes on the farms.

We lived like one family. We turned our wages over and mother took care of the money. She gave us our spending money or a dollar if we were broke.

In Glen Lyon my father-in-law gave me a job as his laborer. We were working three-handed. You would have a miner and he would have two

58

laborers. I labored with him for awhile, then I had a chance to get with a miner and a single laborer-two handed. So I left my father-in-law. You could make a lot more money. But not that much because in Glen Lyon they had a car limit so you could only make so much. Where you would make your extra money is if you put up timber, props and stuff like that. In Mocanaqua you could make money because they would let you load as many cars as you wanted.

⊘ They had a limit in Glen Lyon because the men wanted the mines to last longer. Susquehanna Coal Company ran it but it was the union that wanted the car limit. It was not the coal company. They [company] tried to break the limit but never really did before World War II.

I was out of work for awhile—the 1925 strike. I went to New Jersey and landed a job in a car shop. My godmother lived in Clifton and said, "If you want a job, Joe, come up here. I have a place where you can sleep and go look for a job." The first job I landed was in a printer works. I went there and there were about thirty people waiting for jobs. When the boss arrived I asked him if he needed help. He asked me if I had experience and I said I did. I had heard an "old Polack" mention the word "plinka machine" (meaning print machine). So I said I had worked on a "plinka machine" and he gave me a job turning the crank for a roller which rolled the paper after it went through water. After the strike I came back though because I didn't like the wages there. You were making more money in the mines.

When I returned to Glen Lyon I never cared to become a section foreman. I was always contract mining, driving airways, proving holes. If they wanted to prove a vein, we would find out how far it went and how thick it was. The engineer would send you up and tell you where to set your gangway. They'd give you a line, the laborer would mark it with chalk, and I knew then where to drill my holes. We never had any trouble with the fire bosses either. He would just tell you where he wanted a prop or a timber and you would just put it there. Section foreman would come in to see that the work was done. When a boss told you to do something you did it. As long as you did what you were told there was never any trouble.

I remember once when they had me proving veins. Well, there was an old slope they called the twenty-four slope. That vein was very loose and shell-like. You didn't know where the bottom or the top was—there was so much coal there. I had to drive an airway and put props all around it. Then they wanted to drive breast in there. They sent a man in there to work with me but he didn't know anything. So I went to see a man in Glen Lyon they called the drunk. He drank a lot but he knew more about the vein than anyone else around, to tell the truth. He told me, "Joe, be

59

careful. Don't put too many [drill] holes in it because it will run away on you." I knew then what I had to do. So then the company sent another man in, and he began to fire the many holes. I told them not to keep firing or the vein would run away. About four days later the vein really caved in. So we had to start from the bottom and dig it all out; it all caved in ninety feet below. You just couldn't use as much powder on this one.

I was mining in sixth shaft in Glen Lyon and they wanted me to go move a new vein—to see which direction it went and drive an airway. The general mine foreman told me, "Joe, if you do that for me I won't forget you." So he gave me a good job putting up headings. You could make more money.

But then Red Harvey comes in and he needs another drill hole. He comes to me and said he needed me, that he heard about my work and needed another hole down at number five tunnel. I said, "Mr. Harvey, I did that already here. Give somebody else a chance to do that. I've only got one pair of lungs and that kind of work is awfully dusty; it's pretty bad." But because I didn't go he kept me out of work for seven months. This was around 1930. Then again I got a job back, but when it finished, for nine months I was again out of work. He did that because I wouldn't go down to five tunnel—well my goodness, he was the big boss.

SARNOSKI: For four years I worked as a laborer. In 1924 I started with my brother-in-law in Glen Lyon, No. 6 colliery. But my brother-in-law was a big boozer; he would get the pay, drink, and not come home for two days. Then he said to me, if I won't go drinking with him I won't have a job. He was making nice money, $150 for two weeks. But he wouldn't keep me working steady. Sometimes I wouldn't get a shift when I came to work. The boss asked me, "What the matter, you no working steady?" I said, my brother-in-law fire me. So boss said, get your papers and I give you job as miner. That's a miracle. I went to courthouse on April 1 [1928]—but it was a holiday*—and got my papers. Soletsky, the mine foreman at No. 6, went with me. He was European too, a good man. Some of the men were complaining though. One said, "How come Sarnoski get a job mining? I've been here from Europe fifteen years and I still a laborer." Soletski said, "I put him there, he gonna stay there." Seniority didn't really matter then. You just had to know foreman well or be a very good worker. But I was a hard worker though I just came from Europe.

I got married in 1937 and I thought it was good then to bring home a $20 pay for two weeks. The colliers weren't working all the time. You

*Miners were celebrating the anniversary of the establishment of the eight-hour day.

tried to get on any shift to load your cars. Some miners went home with little on their paychecks after expenses were deducted for powders and laborers.

If you were out of work you go to a priest in Plymouth and you get a job. Even if you were in Glen Lyon he could help you because he was with the companies. He was a stockholder, I think. Some felt Father Lypinsky in Glen Lyon even kept the breaker open in Glen Lyon. It was a holy breaker because it was working six days a week and nobody in the county was working that much in the 1930's. "That's gonna change some day," people said, and the year after he died [1936] they shut the breaker down for remodeling. We were off for six months. In fact, I went back to Europe for four months. Most of the people thought that it was Lypinsky which kept it open because he had shares in it, especially when it closed for a while the year after he died. Lypinsky was pastor with St. Albert's Polish Church.

There used to be a lot of payoffs to foremen for jobs. Some men wanted to get a decent chamber [with easily accessible coal] on a good gangway. They would meet foremen in beer gardens on payday and pay them, buy them drinks. If you got a better place in the mines you could make more money. But you couldn't do nothing about it. If a boss didn't like you you could lose your job. And the union leaders didn't fight it because they were friendly with the company. Union leaders and local officials would be given the best jobs in them days. If you a miner, president of a local, and have two laborers, you could put your bedroom slippers on in the morning and just go and see how your laborers work. And you just give them order what they gonna do and you came home. And you would get more pay than two miners did. This was true at Glen Lyon.

The Glen Alden Coal Company had the most collieries in the valley. And in 1935, when the insurgent miners were active, they had a meeting at Glen Lyon. Frank Shifko of the United Mine Workers told the men to stay with the union and not go with Maloney.* So we voted to stay with the union. Shifko said we would lose our jobs if Maloney would win. I said to myself, I might as well stick with my union. The United Mine Workers was big at that time.

What hurt is that the insurgents couldn't really succeed in Glen Lyon. The union had the iron hand on you. Even when the insurgents had meetings they found out if you attended. I remember one meeting [of the insurgents] at the Roosevelt School. One UMW official went through and

*Thomas Maloney of Wilkes-Barre led a movement called the United Anthracite Miners in 1934 and 1935 which attempted to split from the United Mine Workers, in part because the UMW was felt to be too closely tied to company officials to adequately represent the rank and file and also because Maloney himself had personal feuds with UMW officials in District One.

anybody attending that meeting they would have no job. You keep your mouth shut and you had a job. Also, we were working fairly steady at Glen Lyon and other collieries weren't. So we didn't want to hurt that. So you're looking out for yourself and your family. The union and the bosses worked together. It was the union officers got the better job. At that time you were satisfied if you had a job. My roots was here so I might as well stay here.

The men at Glen Lyon were forced to go with the United Mine Workers. Men were for Maloney but you were afraid to say it. If you support Maloney you would lose your job. The companies supported the union; they cooperated. You could put up timber and they wouldn't even pay you for it if they didn't like you. If they were against you they'd push you out, that's all. If you speak out too much they put a stick and powder on your porch. The leaders of the union were always against Maloney, for they had good jobs with the union and their local was getting $1,200 [share of dues] from the district. We got a leader in Glen Lyon, Stanley Kisinski.* When you go for a job in Glen Lyon you have to see him. If you insulted the president of the local union you wouldn't get a job no place—even at another colliery. The companies would stick together. They would ask where you worked last? Why did you leave your job? They would call and tell you they didn't want you if they got a bad report.

If you were president of the union local at Glen Lyon it was hard for anyone to run against you. My friend, Joe Doris, ran for president and they made him leave town. He had to move to Baltimore. That's the kind of union it was in Glen Lyon. Kisinski was biggest guy in the union there. Nobody could beat him in Glen Lyon. One time the votes were counted and Kisinski lost; they go in the other room and count the votes again and Kisinski win. I knew that good. At some of the elections at the union local they had ballots numbered and a list of numbers so that they could usually tell how you voted.

SUDOL: You had to attend the majority of union meetings if you wanted to run for office. If you never went to the meetings you never know what is going on. They passed a ruling. You had to attend so many meetings to run. If there was a good man they would go along with him but the men were scared. If somebody would say a little too much, the first thing you know he would lose his job. John [Sarnoski] would know; he lost his job. Kisinski gave the foreman orders, "We don't want that man."

SARNOSKI: So, I had to go to another mine to work, and they wouldn't

---

*Name changed at request of respondent.

hire me. They blackballed me. Kisinski was president and if anyone ran against him he was out. They were like a bunch of "Gestapos" in Glen Lyon.

STEWART: In those days the president of the local union and the men on the grievance committee had the best jobs in the colliery. You would see them in the morning always talking with the mine foreman in the offices. That was true all over. If you wanted to get one of these committeemen on your side, all you had to do was "sugar him up," give him one of the better jobs in the mines and he was your baby. If you were a union official and you were supposed to work seven or eight hours a day, it would rain several days a month. But you couldn't find them sometimes. The laborers they had working for them covered up; they wouldn't tell you where they were. If he didn't cover up he wouldn't have a job. That official might be gone home at 10:30 in the morning. His laborer stayed there until 2:30. You take the sections foreman book to the mine foreman and when it came back these union officials would have seven hours. So you'd raise hell about it. I was told more than once, you're lucky you got a job.

SARNOSKI: You know when they had the miners' convention and Kisinski was president, who would go? President, secretary and other officials would go for two weeks. But then laborers would still load their cars and they would still be paid for loading so many cars a day even when they weren't there. And they got the best places in the mines, where the coal was easiest to load. So he was getting money from the local for the convention and when he came back he gonna get paid just like he was working. Figure this out!

SUDOL: At one time Glen Lyon had two locals; things were better. When you put in a grievance things were solved. They had one local for the outside men and one for the men in the mines. I remember good grievance men like Sam Somone. He was good. He'd say right to the boss, "Buddy, you pay this man what he's got coming or this colliery doesn't work."

SARNOSKI: My buddy Joe Doris was running against Kisinski in the 1930's for president of our local. I could hear them counting the votes and I bet Doris was ahead three to one. Then you know what Kisinski done? He said this was too much noise in the hall and with a cop he took them over to the hall to count again. The next day he took the ballots to the district office and a week later they announced Kisinski had won. Figure this out! They wanted to count the votes at the district office. They didn't want the miners to see them. Doris had to move to Balti-

63

more. He could have gotten a job here but it would be in a hole with water where you couldn't stand it very long.

SUDOL: At Glen Lyon in the gangway sometimes you would have to load rock before you could get at coal or put timber up. The gangway was the main road going in. But the union limited you as to how many cars you could load. You could load only so much coal, so much rock, or put up so much timber. But the company complained that they wanted the limit broke so the miners could load more coal. The limit started to break [after World War II] when machinery came in. Other collieries didn't have a limit.

The reason Glen Lyon had a limit on production is so the jobs would last longer, because if you worked in a gangway you would only load four; if you worked in a breast you would load five and go home.

SARNOSKI: The company wanted to break the limit. Before that I would load only five cars, get eight dollars and go home. If I load another five cars the company would pay me less so they were to make more money on all the extra cars I would load. That's how they wanted to break the limit.

Every colliery had its own rate sheet. At the Susquehanna Coal Company [Glen Lyon] they paid more than they paid in Wanamie. The local union at the colliery determined the rates. In the contract they would specify what you got paid for each car loaded and for props. But if you didn't get it in the contract you wouldn't get paid.

STEWART: During the Maloney strike [1934-1935] there was a lot of people that went to work and many were afraid to go to work. You brought insurgents in here. And the State police came in and they were just as bad as the ones that were called out on strike. The State police treated the people even worse than the ones that were trying to break the union. At Wanamie there was a lot of support for the Maloney union because the people got tired of United Mine Workers and what they were doing. The United Mine Workers and the bosses were hand in glove. They were working together. Maloney came in and tried to break that. Men were also mad that some collieries—like Glen Lyon—were working and others were not. They felt here was favoritisms and collusion between union and companies. I remember one Christmas I had two children and only two days' pay in my check.

The insurgents never shut down the Wanamie Colliery, but they tried to shut it down. The thing was that those men who supported Maloney and those who supported the United Mine Workers—they were born and raised together. They were good friends. They [insurgents] didn't want to

Glen Lyon breaker, c. 1937

stop you if you had the guts to go to work; they left you go but they give you a good kick in the ass when you were going.

I was fifty-fifty on Maloney. Some days I went to work and some days I didn't. If I could get away with it, I went to work. When you came home at night they'd be calling you "bluebird" all the way up the street. You didn't know what to do. You would be called bluebird or seal. Like I say, I just turned my head the other way and went to work. The next day you'd go outside and you'd feel bad. There'd be one guy standing at the bottom of your steps and another standing down the road. Rather than run through them you would join them. A couple days after if you wanted to go to work the door was always open to go.

Stanley Salva

Born in 1905 to parents who had emigrated from Galicia, Stanley Salva entered the coal mines of Glen Lyon, Pennsylvania and eventually played an influential role in the affairs of its United Mine Workers of America local. He revealed clearly how communities moved to protect their jobs and the intricate system of relationships between workers and local union officials. In Glen Lyon, control over the workplace was not a simple struggle between labor and capital but involved a more complex relationship which included union officials as well.

I started working at the coal breaker at thirteen years of age. In those days if you weren't fourteen yet and started working you had to go to continuation school one day a week. You started picking slate. But when I was seventeen I drove mules in the mines. Sometimes I would put sprigs of wood under coal cars to slow them down. That was called nipping. Eventually I started laboring at the Susquehanna Coal Company in Glen Lyon. The company was really owned by the M. A. Hanna Company in Cleveland. They owned soft-coal mines too. Around here they owned mines in Glen Lyon, Shamokin and Nanticoke.

You had to work hard but you didn't mind it because you were young and able. As a young man it was a practice that as soon as you were old enough and strong enough you went into the mines and made money. That's what I wanted. Not many were concerned about leaving the community and going elsewhere. The only time people left was when they closed the breaker down for repairs in 1936 for six months. They put new equipment in the breaker in 1936. That's a time when lots of people left. Some went to Detroit to automobile factories. Some never came back.

I labored for a long time with my father. You had to get mining papers to be a miner and you couldn't get them until you worked in the mines at least two years. Eventually my father got older and said to the boss, "I will labor for my son now if you make him the miner." I actually worked inside the mines for thirty years and another twenty-five years outside the mines. My parents wanted me to stay in school longer than I did. But you knew that they would be unable to afford your going to school and not working. You had to make your own money.

In 1925 we were on strike. A few of us guys decided to go to New Jersey to get jobs for a while. I worked in a freight station in Patterson where my aunt lived. But I came back [after the strike] because my mother and father were here. Even the company expected you would come back and work for them again.

Once we started to work after 1925 it was steady. During the depression, in fact, Glen Lyon kept on working. We worked so steady we were mentioned in Ripley's "Believe it or Not." Yet, in Nanticoke the same company didn't work a full week. They had a lot of slack time. Every once in a while we might have a day or two off. And the mines would never work on Polish holidays: Three Kings' Day, Christmas Day and St. Joseph's Day. The company never had no objection, although as time went on they didn't like it because they wanted to sell more coal. In other words people were pretty religious.

In Glen Lyon the union local had put a limit on production. In order to distribute the cars evenly they kept it for a long time. For instance, if you had a good place to work [coal was easily accessible] the company used to allow you to fill more cars because you could load faster. But that wasn't fair. So what we decided was you couldn't load more than was required for a normal day's pay. In most of the places it was five cars a day. In some gangways it was four. In easier places maybe you only had three as a limit. If you were over the limit you would pay a fine. We wanted everyone to have an equal load and pay. We had to watch that the boss might not let a "pet" of his load more cars than the other guy and make the coal last longer.

Hell, some bosses played favorites. They could give you better places to work, easier jobs. Every place in the mines is not alike. In some place you would have to work harder than in others to produce coal. A boss could get money if he did you a favor. It was hard to prove but the men knew about it. You met a boss at the bar and made sure he got his free drinks. Lots of them did that.

I belonged to the union right after I started working. I held offices like auditor and later president of the local. We used to have three locals in Glen Lyon. They were all under the United Mine Workers. At that time [1920-1930] they figured they had to have one for the miners, one for the company hands, and one for the outside employees. I joined the local for the outside employees at first, when I worked in the breakers. After 1930 the national office wanted us to do away with our three groups and have one local. But the locals for the miners and company hands wouldn't surrender and they remained separate. But we had joint meetings by 1935 and I became president of both. One reason was because I could speak Polish good and most of the men were Polish or Slavish [Slovak].

If the company didn't treat us right we went out on strike. The company had a rate sheet or schedule of wages which differed from the colliery. When I was on the grievance committee of our local I had to put pressure on the company to get copies of the rate sheet. I would also get mad when companies would try to hire some of their friends from out of town or some boss would hire his friends in. A union leader could stop a man from getting a job. In the 1930's we made sure that the people in Glen Lyon got jobs first. If you lived elsewhere you couldn't get a job in Glen Lyon while I was president. We would just tell the foreman he wasn't allowed to hire him and he would listen. They were afraid of shutdowns.

We also had a problem when the company would dock the pay of men who they said were loading too much refuse in the cars. We had to reach an agreement that a man would be allowed at least five hundred pounds of refuse in a car. He wouldn't be penalized for that. Maybe a miner would have sixty cars of coal loaded during a period but they would pay him for fifty and dock him ten cars for rock and refuse. I fought that.

Sometimes a miner would try to pay me for a better spot to mine where he could get better production. One man and his buddy were working an area and tried to offer me money so he would be permitted to load coal from two places, taking away part of the coal from the man working next to him. He had thought we would favor him because he had given me ten dollars once when I was running for school director. But we [the grievance committee] wouldn't take no money off him, and we ruled that two men would continue to work in the same place, with the tonnage evenly split.

As a union official you could help a man get a job or a different job once in a while. You could see the foreman or fire boss or even the general foreman. He mostly had all the authority so you kind of talked to him. He usually didn't want to see no trouble and he wanted to be on the right side of the union. At Glen Lyon, I talked to Bill Harvey, the general mine foreman. They were all Welsh—never any Poles. In fact, after the first World War, when no one could get a job in the mines, the Welsh could come over and have a job while still on the boat. Our people couldn't get a job and the Welsh came right in and settled heavily in Nanticoke and this valley. And when we forced only the hiring of men from Glen Lyon [Poles and Slovaks] we stopped the Welsh from coming from Nanticoke.

Most of the bosses had been brought in from Shamokin, where the Susquehanna Coal Company had their first mines. They brought their experienced men here and some would bring their relations from Wales.

Ben Grevera and Anthony Piscotty

Ben Grevera was born in Nanticoke in 1913 of parents from the Ger-man-controlled sectors of Poland. He worked for the Susquehanna Col-lieries for nearly a lifetime. His friend Anthony Piscotty was born nearby in Plymouth in 1908. He worked at the Loomis Colliery, where he was a strong supporter of the United Anthracite Miners Union.

GREVERA: I was born in the city of Nanticoke, and grew up here all my life. Been around here all my life in Nanticoke. I'll go back to the time my dad came from Germany. Come to this country when he was about eight years old. Nine years old he started working the breakers, nine hours a day for a quarter a day. And from the breaker, as a young man, he went in the mines for Susquehanna Collieries for fifty-three years. Just in this one colliery. And when he got older—this is the history of my father—he asked for a lighter job, 'cause he couldn't do any mine work or working in the cold. They told him that they had paid him for what he had done. My old dad had to quit work. Later on, I went into coal mines. I mined coal and I mined in the gangways. My people were taken from Prussia into Germany. That's where they were raised. My dad was only a boy, eight years old anyway, when he come here. And my mother's fam-ily came from the same country—Prussia to Germany and back here. When my brothers got older they started work around the colliery. One brother worked on the outside as a shaftsman, and the other three boys, they went in the mines. One worked in rock tunnels and then he went on to coal. I started to work in the mines. I was about twenty-five years old. I lived with my father-in-law. We were getting eighteen dollars a week, and I was giving him five dollars a week to help him out too.

Before that I was with my dad, working on a truck. I worked for an ice cream service too. My mother was dead. She died when I was fourteen years old. She had a stroke. So after my mom died, then my brothers started leaving to get married. So me and Dad was alone. I used to love when I first started—what take was I getting? Seven dollars a week on the ice truck, and seven days a week. I'd come home with that pay to my dad, he'd give you a quarter to spend. Then later on, as I worked down there, I got old enough to drive the truck. Then I went and I was getting $18 a week, I think. Before I got married.

Q: Now, then you don't really start in the mines till the late thirties, right?

GREVERA: Well, '37, I'd say. Around 1937. Somewhere around there. Seventeen years I stayed in the mines. Then I got out, 'cause I have third-stage asthma. I had to get out of the mine. I drove gangways in rock, not just in coal alone. But the gangways you drove in rock and you blow this rock out. Then you'd get your road in, then you drained your top vein; that's where the coal was. Fire this coal out, cleaned the coal out, then you had maybe six, seven feet of rock again to blow up. This is what they called a gangway. We'd go in there sixty, fifty feet, then you'd drive a chute up for ventilation. Before you'd get this ventilation in there, the air that you used for jackhammers to drill [was all you had]. You'd have the hose in there to get air for you to breathe. This is how you had to go. Later on, they come up with the respirator. But then I couldn't use them, because I couldn't breathe with it on. I was really closed up with asthma.

Q: Did you, before you even went in the mines, did you ever say, "Hey, I'm not going to go in there?" You saw how your father suffered.

GREVERA: I said, "I'll never go in the mines and get sick like my father." My four uncles—that's my father's brothers—died with asthma. My dad died with it. And I says, "I'll never go in there." When I got married, well, what was there left? I had to go in and make a living. There was no other way out. I didn't have enough education. Well, I guess you could leave the area, but I didn't have any intentions of leaving home. 'Cause my dad had the home there and left his home to me after he died. And I stayed with him, so I didn't want to leave home. And then I had children after I got married. And I wasn't going to go away from here. And I still live in the same room. All the brothers and all, we were born and raised in that home. It was a company home. They used to pay six dollars and a quarter a month rent.

Q: And did your father have a chance to own it finally?

GREVERA: Yes. When the coal company sold the property, they had the first choice—1928 or '29. We didn't have too much of this.

Q: Now you were living in Plymouth yet? Right? Why did your father want you to leave the Chauncey?

PISCOTTY: There was three of us there: there was too many from one family. Then he had two of his first cousins. The boss said to him, "Joe, you got too many working from the family." So I said, "I'll get a job over at Loomis," and I worked there eleven years. My father was born here. His grandfather come from Poland. He worked up in the Grand Tunnel too—he used to work up there [before] he come here. His name was Mike. Of course my dad was a big man. I'm the smallest one in the family. He was a strong man. He didn't have too much education.

Q: What about some of your other brothers and sisters—did they have to go to work early as well? And where did they go?

PISCOTTY: Yeah. My brother George. He worked for Chauncey. When it closed down, then he come to Susquehanna and worked in the breaker. Then he left. He went to Chester. He was working for a concern down there; he was a tool man or something. Took care of all of their plumbing and stuff down in Chester. He's retired now. He's older than I. The next brother, Mike, he's in Plymouth. He worked in the mines. He used to work with Benny in the mines; he was a rock man. He was in bad shape, but exercises sort of helped that asthma. You'd be surprised how that helps, you know, that exercise. So Mike is still living at home. He got himself a home, and a flood came down and made a mess out of it in 1972, so he built him a home there. Of course Uncle Sam helped, you know, helped fix it up.

Q: Your sisters as young girls, did they have to work in any of the mills around here?

PISCOTTY: Yeah, they worked in the mills. One sister is still single, she still lives in Plymouth. My sister Louise—Lizzy—she's away from here. John had got two liquor stores out in Connecticut. Chester is a tool man out in Niagara Falls. He works out there. My father took care of all the men. He set everything, he fixed up, done all the repair work at night. Every night there was so much things to do, and if the machine wasn't running right, he'd had to see that it was fixed up, take care of her. And the breaker, that's regular mechanic. That's just like being a mechanic, see. He could take care of it. He started me off when I was a youngster, showed me how to lay the sheet iron, how to cut it, what to do, how to do it. When I went to Loomis, I was tops.

Q: And that would wear out once in a while?

PISCOTTY: Sure, that wears out. It wears out fast, and you'd have to keep repairing it and keep it going so they wouldn't block up your chute. When you've got the stuff coming in from the mines, you can't stop that; you gotta keep this thing rolling. Everybody's working, everybody's getting paid, you gotta keep making money for the people. If you don't, then they don't need you. You know that goes today. You gotta produce. Well, that's what it was them days. I know my dad told me that when he started in the breaker he was about eight years old. When he'd come over and the boss'd find a piece of slate by the floor and he'd kick in their ears, and whack it. It's true. They used to do that to my dad quite a number of times. But, he did a fine job, my dad. I guess he must have worked till he worked the breaker down. He worked, they tore the breaker down, and that was it. That was quite a number of years. I just forgot what year that Chauncey was closed down. In 1940 [or] something, around in there.

Q: What do you start to do at Loomis? What's your job there, and how long do you stay in there?

PISCOTTY: Slate picker. I start off as a slate picker. See, when you work the breaker them days, and if you were a worker—if you were a man that wanted to work overtime—you got all you wanted and the boss always took you in. And I used to love to work. I think I worked there the third day and the boss foreman says, "Would you like to sweep up tonight?" And I told him, "Sure." "Well," he said, "you come out every night," and I worked every night. And make yourself some extra bucks, you know. So that's how you got on. Later on I became a shaker tender, then I was a washery boss. Loomis had a washery. I was washery boss there for quite a number of years. Then I come back to the breaker. Of course that was the top place, because I was a union man, see. They said I could have job at the breaker back when they closed the washery down. I worked there till the strike—1935—when we all lost our job at that time. They'd have listened to me, they'd have went in the mines, they'd stayed in the mines—nobody'd worked. We'd have worked the strike. Just like they done in Poland. When they go on strike, they stay in the mines. Try to get us to do something. They'd have done it that time; I told [Thomas] Maloney to do it. I was surprised when the strike broke out. They could have killed them that time.

Q: I've heard a lot of the men who were in the union, who worked in the breakers or worked in the mines, who said that they felt the union [UMW] officials weren't always working as hard for the men and that they were perhaps too close to the companies. Was that true? Do you think that the companies had a real grip on the union officials here in the '20's, '30's, '40's?

PISCOTTY: Some locals weren't too good. Some people wanted to fight for you, they'd fight for you. You take in our place at the Loomis up there, we had—Tormaf, he was the president of our local. And we fought them at that time. I think at that time we were going pretty good. But, see, we were always having trouble. They would turn around and they would fire a good guy just so you'd have a strike. Well they don't want to take him back and we wouldn't go to work, so we'd go on strike. This thing happened off and on. You should see that; you should have been around. The State troopers used to come out and boy they used to club us.

GREVERA: Well I was a mine official. I mean a union official.

Q: What was your position?

GREVERA: Committeeman. I was one guy stuck with the men, and I had hell holes to work in. If I'd have listened to the coal company and done what they wanted me to do, I'd have been the boss in a coal company and taken care of. But I wouldn't. They wanted you to see that the men loaded more coal for the same wages, and I wouldn't go along with it. We had a contract to live up to, and that's what I lived up to, the contract that they agreed on—yardage, the price of a car of coal. The minute they wouldn't pay, I was after them. They even offered me to go to school, that I'd be taken care of, but I refused.

Q: What type of school did they want to send you to?

GREVERA: To be a mine foreman. We were talking about our dads working in the breaker. My dad and his [Piscotty] dad, they got a licking from the boss in the breaker and they'd come home and they were crying that the boss give them a licking. Their mother or dad'd give them another licking for not listening to the boss. That's how tough it was. And they were only—like he said, his father [was] eight, my dad was nine years old. They couldn't come home crying, because they got another licking.

Q: Could a union official at Susquehanna get better work if he was a little bit more cooperative?

GREVERA: With the company? Yes, yes. There was a lot of it, but I was one guy wouldn't sell myself. I always said, I was elected by the people, and I stayed with the people. But in the windup, I wound up with third-stage asthma.

PISCOTTY: Well, at Loomis during the '30's most people supported the insurgent miners and Tom Maloney at that time. Understand the way they are. They had a checkoff, and we were doing away with checkoff, we were collecting—I happened to be a secretary-treasurer from the outside when I worked there. See, I was a union man too for the UMW. Well sometimes you get one day, sometimes you get two more or less. It was like anything else. We get a pay for four days and then some of the other collieries that was with them, they'd be working every day. And it was again with the United Mine Workers. I was one of them [insurgents]. We closed it [Loomis Colliery] down. But then after a couple of weeks, this gang—our buddies here—they battled us. These guys was battling us. So, if they'd have listened to me and went in the mines and struck in the mines, and stayed down in the mines, we'd have won the strike. But they didn't want to do that. We wanted to go down to the foot of the shaft in the mines and stay there and see who'd come down and get us to come out. You know you have about two hundred men down there, or three hundred—we'd have won the strike. But they didn't want to listen at that time. He was afraid to take that chance. He was afraid that the people on the outside would get hysterical. My wife, his wife, everybody in on this, would leave. We'd stay down there.

Q: What did you hope to accomplish? What were your objectives in this strike, in this effort [1935]?

PISCOTTY: At that time, to get the men back that was fired or that got the works put to them like. Maybe they laid off certain guys or they didn't pay certain people—they owed them money. That's what we used to strike for. But they didn't keep work balanced off right. If they would get us all equal working time it would have been all right. But some collieries, worked four, five days a week. Some of the other collieries would work every day. Over in Hazelton, those Glen Alden collieries, they worked every day, you know; that wasn't fair. Some guys had them big, and some of them starting—making them like this [gesturing], like hay wagons. That's what they were starting to do at the Loomis. That was our problem. We tried to tell them that there was more goes in there and we want more money for that car. They wouldn't give them to you. They'd say that your car—and you were a poor man—they'd take your car out there and they'd say it was all slate, wouldn't pay for it. I knew Maloney. Tom Maloney worked at the Stanton Colliery up in Wilkes-Barre. We made him the leader. *We* elected him as the president of the United Anthracite Miners. The vice-president, secretary, treasurer, everybody—we elected them. We formed our own union. Tom was a good speaker, and he was always battling for the men when we were working at United Mine Workers. He was the one calling the strikes, and we'd follow suit. So we couldn't do nothing with the United Mine Workers, so then we formed a new union. These fellows, they were OK down there.

Q: So really you had two sources of grievances, then. One was you weren't working as much, and secondly you weren't being treated fairly.

GREVERA: That's right. Well, I was one guy against them [the company]. That's what I say, when I went against them. I worked in a hell hole. They either put you in rock, or I worked in a place down in two shafts. You'd go to work, sit down—they'd have your breakfast—I wheeled coal out of the place. They worked you. Thirty feet from the gangway—that's the main road—to the face we'd load wheelbarrow of coal, come out, throw the coal into the car. I was soaking wet till quitting time. And I would load three cars a day and put the timber up. Then the superintendent comes down and says to me, you should load more coal. And I was on the mine committee then, a committeeman. And I says to the superintendent, "Here's my lamp, now give me your book and your light. Now you go and take that wheelbarrow and go and get that coal out of there." He says, "No way." "Well," I says, "so long." And I quit working. I was out for three weeks. They tried to get me back to work and I wouldn't go back. A neighbor of mine was a mine foreman, Mr. Ball. He says to the head mine foreman, "Why don't you give me that man? I'll give him a job in my section." He says, "You'll never have him, he's a tough man." He says, "Well, just give me him." So he agreed to give me a job with this Mr. Ball. I went to work with him and he never had any trouble. They put me on the day base. Loaded my coal, I'd go home. I'd worked for months already, and the big guy called Mr. Ball, and he says, "How's he doing?" "I have no trouble with him. Load his coal every day, loads his shift," [the foreman said]. "I have no trouble," he says, "I give him his orders and he goes in and does his work, and that's it."

PISCOTTY: I was the head of this Nanticoke section here.

Q: For the Anthracite Miners?

PISCOTTY: Yeah, I was fighting these guys. My buddies, now they're all my buddies. I was the secretary-treasurer from the outside. I was there in the United Mine Workers, and I was the same thing when I took over in the Anthracite Miners. I took the same job, because I could see my way clear to staying with these guys. They [the UMW] weren't doing nothing for us. They're taking our money, they're taking our checkoff out of our pay, and they weren't doing anything for us. See, the checkoff was one of the worst things that ever happened to you. And I knew Jennings too. He was a printer here. He stuck up for the UAM because he seen what was going on. So they tried to impeach him. They took him down, they tried to blame him for blowing up Judge Valentine's car during the Maloney trial. They tried to blame that poor bugger for it. My God, he didn't know nothing about it. He was a nice guy. They tried to frame him on it.*

Q: Why did they pick out Jennings? Just because he supported the Anthracite Miners?

PISCOTTY: Yeah, yeah. He was a businessman. He helped.

*Emerson Jennings owned a small print shop in Wilkes-Barre and was accused of planting a bomb in the car of Judge W. A. Valentine on March 28, 1935 while Valentine was presiding over a trial of Thomas Maloney and other United Anthracite Miners' officials for disregarding a strike injunction. The American Civil Liberties Union investigated the case and concluded that Jennings was framed by Luzerne County and Glen Alden officials.

PISCOTTY: I was born in Plymouth, 1908. I worked at the Chauncey. First I started off at the Chauncey as a breaker boy, just a little colliery on the other side of the river. Chauncey owned it. My dad was the breaker boss. About thirteen I had to go to continuation school one day a week—see, I was too young. I think we had more dust in that breaker, that you couldn't see your hand in front of you. See, in them days they didn't have it like they do today. They wet the stuff before it comes up and it's harder of course to clean. When it's dry, it's easier to clean, only you have all that dust. I was a brakeman, that's about it. So I worked there for I guess about three or four years. The breaker burned down while I was working there. The breaker burned down, you know, my dad was still a breaker boss. My brother was running the engine up there. He's pulling cars up. They build a new breaker. So I was a boiler room tender. I had a good job then, boiler room tender. So after I got back into the breaker, my dad said to me one day, "You know, Tony, your brother's working here, you're working here. Why don't you go get a job somewhere else?" I said, "Why sure, I'll get a job. I'll go over to the Loomis and I'll hire myself." Never asked why, just sent in the stuff and got myself hired, and I was working there. I don't know how many years I worked there—now let's see—I must have worked there eleven, twelve years at the Loomis. It was during suspension hours there, 1925 strike, when you had that. That was a long suspension you had along there. That was six months. Yeah, that was the longest we ever had. I remember them days very well because after working these number of years, that suspension, we used to build bunks, play cards all night, and in the morning go to the shedding shanty and take yourself a bath and go to sleep, sleep all day. Yeah, because we were on strike. That's what we used to do. I remember the days: I'd get me a loaf of bread, and some butter—we had cows—butter and some milk and coffee; that's what you got. That was it for the whole day.

Q: Where was he from? Wilkes-Barre?

PISCOTTY: Yeah. He'd take us to Harrisburg—wouldn't cost us any-thing—buy us a meal. You'd have to testify down there. So I testified down there before the representatives on that.

Q: Who else supported the Anthracite Miners? Anyone else in the com-munity, or was it tough to get support?

PISCOTTY: Well, a lot of people supported us, but they were afraid to come out and say it. You take down this section, it was different.

Q: Where? In Nanticoke?

PISCOTTY: Yeah, in Nanticoke section it was a little different. This side you mostly worked here over to Bliss Colliery or up through the Loomis or maybe some collieries here or Buttonwood. We're right in the middle here. Then after we left there, 1935—February 2 was the last day I worked there.

Q: At the Loomis? Why?

PISCOTTY: Well, yes. After we got pushed out you just pushed out. They wanted to give me a job as riffraff in the mines—the bosses, when I went up to see them for a job. I took my son with me at that time. He was only about seven years old. So I took my son up there. They was carrying a couple of guys out of the mines. He said, "Dad, you're not going to go into the mines again are you?" So I turned around and go home and I never went back. I went into business. I went into the tavern business. I owned a tavern business and I made a success out of it.

Q: What about the—say in the Nanticoke area—some of the people within the community, let's say the priests in the Polish churches, or something like that. Did they ever take public stands towards the union or the companies or Maloney?

PISCOTTY: They weren't allowed to. Some of the priests might have said something like half the men was working, the other half wasn't working. If you were in their position, what would you do? You going to put your neck out here? For what? You couldn't very well do it.

Coal miners' bar, Glen Lyon, c. 1925

PISCOTTY: I was in the tavern business twenty-nine years and something. Twenty-nine years, pretty near thirty years. Miners always come in and fraternize. I remember there was about fifteen, sixteen of them used to come in. They had good money, you see. How about helping us out? Who's running? Give me the slate. And as my friends come in I had about—I don't want to tell you, that's one thing I can't tell you, what you do.

GREVERA: People were being made to listen to you, 'cause you were on a committee and like a business place. You'd have these people coming in having to drink in your place. Well, what do you say, give this fellow a nod, he's running for office. A good man. Same thing when you come in, he's in the union. Well, you've asked them to help out, and this is how it would go. Help them out a lot. This is how these towns operated. It's who you knew and people that worked with you.

PISCOTTY: The Round Up Inn, used to call it. The Round Up Inn. Then I changed it to Piscotty's after. They would say, "You're not a cowboy, you better change it to Piscotty's Place."

GREVERA: They did have men like bosses and that played ball with the politicans. If they wanted somebody in office, that boss would go to the workers in the mines and look, you go along with this fellow. If you don't you're out. And that's how they played ball. Well, election day proved that. That's how you know anytime if the people are with you or not. The count of the last ballot, and then they know if you were with them or not. And if you weren't with them, they lost their election. You was out.

PISCOTTY: That was the old saying. You'd come out of the mines and you'd go to the bar and say, "Give me a shot in the beer." That was a miner's drink. Couple of shots and beers and away you'd go, and come back.

Q: Did the coal companies have much of an influence on the town or the town government? Some people have said that before World War II especially, and even later, many other companies would have located in this region, but the coal companies, who owned most of the land, kept them out.

PISCOTTY: They owned it all.

GREVERA: They owned it all. The people who owned it come in here and they wouldn't allow it to be sold. No other companies could come in here because the coal companies figured they'd lose the workers.

PISCOTTY: All them years we fought. I've been on the council here in town, we built a shoe factory and put in money. They didn't opposed the shoe factory. The shoe factory was when the monies was gone, most of the money. '45 they were starting to get out. The Susquehanna went out in 1952.

GREVERA: The youngest people started to leave in '54, '55 because there was no work. The only place they had to work was like Tony said, the shoe factory.

Q: How did that affect your business?

PISCOTTY: The business? Well, I told you what happened. When the Susquehanna closed down here, I went to the Loomis. The Loomis was still working. I got my friends there to patronize down this way.

Q: Mr. Grevera, when did you finally stop working in the mine?

GREVERA: 1954.

Q: When the colliery closed?

GREVERA: Yeah.

Q: Were you old enough to retire then?

GREVERA: No, I went out to work in a cigar mill; I worked getting $52 a week. Watchman. Made money, working steady—midnight—there. I worked there about seven, eight years. Then I went over and got a job up in the warehouse in Wilkes-Barre as a watchman. I worked there for a few years. Later on I got a job for the State highway department on the road. I retired in 1969. I couldn't work anyway. I took sick and went to a doctor and took x-rays and that's when I found out that I had third-stage asthma. When I went back to the doctor he says to me, "Ben, you can't work no more, you got third-stage asthma."

William Everett

William Everett had a unique perspective on activities in the northern anthracite fields during the 1930's. He was a foreman for the Glen Alden Coal Company at the Loomis Colliery between 1934 and 1935 and served in a similar capacity at the Truesdale Colliery from 1935 to 1939. He provides rich detail on the manner in which companies like Glen Alden attempted to control the direction and extent of labor protest during the strikes which shook the region during the depression decade.

EVERETT: The men were fighting among themselves; some would work and some wouldn't work. I had one colored guy by the name of Reggie Lewis—a powerful man. He loved the ground I walked on. One morning I·was riding to work on street car with Lewis. "Bill, don't get on that next car. They done attacked us," he said, but I went on anyway. Finally the car stopped for a man with a lunch pail but he was only a decoy. Once the car stopped the nuts and bolts started to fly at the car. Windows broke. I ducked. All the "niggers" on the car was—but they ducked down with me. Everyone of them had a revolver.

The next road down. It was a bad neighborhood. There was a girl getting ready for work. She left her dressing table for a while; when she returned from the bathroom there was a bullet hole right in the mirror she had been looking into.

Pretty soon the State police came and took the car to work. Most of the Negroes were imported as strikeworkers by Glen Alden. We had a guy in New York who was getting so much a head for sending them up here—white and black, anything he could get.

[During the 1934 strike Glen Alden actually had Everett move into a small company house for a while to be in closer contact with the men.]

Handling the men. One day a young laborer working for me put a log on trucks to disrupt car. So the following day when he came to work I went right down to his place and told him, "Tomorrow morning you put a log across that road when you're coming and you're alone and see what happens." Another time this same guy led a gang of fifty or sixty men to colliery to close it down. There were some shots exchanged with company police. So I came out and saw this gang on our property [and I went down and confronted them]. The main grievances of men on strike that they were working only two, three days a week.

When I became a General Superintendent I met with a committee for all of the collieries. The first thing they said to me was, "Listen Everett, we heard all about you [at South Wilkes-Barre Colliery]. When you were at Loomis, you were the boss of the Loomis local. When you were at

Truesdale you were the boss at the Truesdale local." They meant that I ran the union as well as the mines.

I will give you an example. I had a foreman at Wanamie who was never loyal to the company. His son was just like him and he was a foreman at the Bliss. One day General Superintendent called me and said that he had seen an application for this man. And we had all been told never to hire this "son of a bitch." So I said, send him into my office tomorrow. When he came in I said, "You know what a *radical* this man was. Why did you hire [someone] like him?" I knew he was really interested in his daughter. "You were looking out for your own reasons. I'm transferring you to Baker Colliery in Scranton [farther from home, making it difficult to get to work]." And I said, "If I ever hear why you were transferred from any source you're gonna be cut off a job. So you might as well know that now. Now you do it. If I ever hear it from any source." He was transferred for attempting to hire this radical. Luckily the Superintendent had caught this. Of course, the boys all figured out why he was transferred but I never heard the reason.

You would hear about men in the area. You knew who was a good man or radical if you were close to the men. All I had to hear was that you were always the leader of the band in a strike situation and I wouldn't hire you. Because I didn't believe in strikes.

Truesdale breaker

81

I'll give you an example. When I went to Truesdale I had a man named Mike Savilich. He had a gangway but he was head of the [Maloney] union committee at Truesdale. So there was a guy, a Greek from Hanover, and he didn't know mining from his ass. But the new union was strong in Hanover and they were pushing for a job for this Greek.

Meanwhile I said to Savilich to meet me down at the pump house one night. But he never showed up. So down to Hanover I go and knocked on his door after midnight. So I went in and I said, "You got a good job, you're making good money." But his wife interrupted, "He's not going to do a thing for you. You might as well know it now." I told her, "I'll tell you something, dear lady, I'm gonna cut his pay in half." She says, "You do and that place will be tied up."

Now Savilich worked on a group where they divided up pay for all the yardage they mined and the timbers they erected. They needed capable men as miner, laborer, and timberman and the Greek would be a disaster on their gang.

So if you had a lousy shifter his pay would be cut in half. Now he had this Spaniard in his gang. The Greek was a good candymaker but as a miner he would be a flop. So I took the Spaniard, who I liked, and put him on a gangway that was so long he could have finished his life down there.

So I told the motormen to deliver the Greek and his tools to Savilich. Before, Savilich claimed he was one of the best men, but when he got him did he ever complain.

After one day I went to Savilich's house and his wife was crying. I said, "Madam, I told you what I was going to do and I did it." Savilich said, "I can't do anything because they have it on record that the man I put on there was a good man."

You see, you had to know how to handle people, you had to manipulate them.

"When I went to No. 3 shift we had a fellow named Torma who was president of the local union and a commissioner for the township. I went to the shaft one morning and I didn't know if we were going to work in the place or not. Torma knew that as mine foreman he would be wise to do something for me. But he decided to get wise and give me the business. So I decided to wait my opportunity [to get even]. Now my office was underground and it was as warm in the winter as it was in the summer because I had heat piped down. Right behind my office was the machinist office. I walked in there one day and here were these guys trying to work in the cold with their noses running. And there was a fellow, which was a helper, and I said, "There's no heat in this shanty. Don't you do a goddamn thing until you run a line into my office. I want some steam in here and heat this goddamn place." So now what have I got? I've got two friends. And one of the guys came from that same neighborhood as Torma and his brother was. So I said to him one day, you want to do me a favor? At the next [union local] meeting when he [Torma] stands up to speak, you stand up and say, "Get out of that goddamn chair or I will throw you out. And he will get out." So he came back to me a few days later and said, "Jesus Christ, Bill, you were right." So he [Torma] lost the presidency of the local.

He could have been half decent to me. He had two grievance committeemen working for me and he must have known what kind of guy I was. [At Loomis] I had this guy and friend start a fight with Torma supporters every time they would come up to vote in election [for Commissioner]. Then State police would come and quiet things down, but then all of his friends were afraid to come and vote. When the votes were counted he lost. He lost both jobs. I put manners in him.

When I was at Truesdale I straightened Savilich out and now this guy.

At Truesdale Victor Matusa [from Nanticoke] was the "brains" of Maloney union at Truesdale. After I got Savilich straightened out I went down to his house one night. "Victor," I said, "what makes you a radical?" "Bill," he says, "my father worked for years at Truesdale and he got nothing. Father was in a 'Catholic place' at Truesdale [a place where they had to carry the coal out like Christ carried the cross]." So I promised I would get him [father] a better place to work. But I asked for one promise, "If you're having trouble of any kind, you sit down with me. And if I can't show you a better way to handle a problem than striking, then you go ahead and strike. So the next day I changed his father. Matusa then trusted me and we got along. Later when Matusa had a son born with club feet he felt he couldn't afford a doctor for the boy, but I sent him to a physician in Wilkes-Barre who was chief surgeon of Glen Alden. He went to doctor and corrected boy's feet and it didn't cost him anything. When Matusa got asthma bad and couldn't go underground, I got him a company job.

Labor, Business and Politics

Vincent Znaniecki

Vincent Znaniecki was born in 1903 in Nanticoke and eventually entered business pursuits in the community. He recounts here not only his career but the experiences of his brothers in the mining regions, some of whom were forced to leave the area for work.

He also reveals the supportive ties between parents and children which often lasted a lifetime, and even the political workings of leaders like John Fine and the coal companies themselves.

ZNANIECK: My father was born in Prussia. It was part of Poland that was taken over by Germany. He lived there, got married there. He was in the German army for about four years. I guess the conditions weren't too favorable. They were unhappy, so they decided to leave and come to America. They first went to La Salle, Illinois. He had some brothers there and friends. So he did get work at the Elgin Watch Company. I don't know what he did there. He was Ignatz. Ignatz Znaniecki. And my mother's name was Veronica Znaniecki. They didn't stay there too long, a few years. I was born in Nanticoke. I have a couple of brothers who were born out there at that time. But the rumors there were that the coal mines were booming and people were getting jobs and earning a little better money than I guess even in the factory. So they left La Salle and come to Nanticoke. My father and mother and the two children. They came together. They met in Europe, were married in Europe and then they came here together. There were some friends and relatives here. I think there was a family by the name of Ship. I don't remember the others, but they were friends—very close friends, even from their days in Poland. So they encouraged them to come here knowing that they could get employment—and they did. Looking back now, of course, they were all fearful of the mines. They knew that the dangers were there, that it wasn't an easy way to make a living, and that they had to work long hours. They weren't paid too much in those days. Oh sure, they all had that fear. Later on, in my days, I went in there for a couple of years when I went to school. I worked night shift, so I knew what the mines were like and what they were doing. I could appreciate. Sure, they were all scared because they had many accidents and nobody to take care of them. If they were hurt, they were on their own. Their friends talk to the bosses, friends that are already working in the mines. They'd talk to the boss and say, "Well, I have another friend, Ignatz Znaniecki; he's came here and he needs work." And that's the way they got work because work was plentiful. The mines were actually just booming, they were starting to boom in those early days. That continued until the first World War. Up until about 1932, why this was a booming area. In my time, when I was a child, they didn't make loads of money. They made enough to live. And the people in those days were very conservative. If they made a few dollars, they were always able to save a dollar out of that, because they always had that fear of uncertainty. And rightfully so. They didn't have any pensions, they didn't have any unemployment insurance. They had nothing. If they didn't save a few dollars, they had nothing. So for that reason they were very, very strict with their money. They used it wisely.

I was born in 1903 in a nice little home up in the Honeypot section. In fact, they call it the Eagle's Nest. It was a home right near the river. The area was beautiful as far as kids were concerned. Plenty of space, there were fields, and the river where we could fish and swim and play. It was very nice, but there wasn't enough money. We didn't live like well-to-do people around.

The Susquehanna Coal Company. In that area, Susquehanna owned everything. Glen Alden started way down here in this section of the town [north end], from the armory out this way to Alden. But it was a beautiful life, the parents were happy and the children were happy. We were poor, you handed down things from one to another. If you got a bicycle, why, everybody in the family used it, and you'd keep repairing it. The same way with sleds in the winter. In a way it was a happy life. There were different nationalities there. There were Polish, Slovak, German and English. That's about it, but it was a friendly situation. They all worked together and they got along. They just seemed like they needed one another, and as a result they helped one another. If someone for instance—if he needed work, they all went together and tried to work with him. If they were in trouble, they would come next in walk and help out in any way they can. If you were sick, they came in and helped. They'd bring in food or clothing or help with the fires or something of that sort. It was a beautiful situation in a way. They were happy in those circumstances, that you would have to make yourself happy there. You know, they couldn't buy it. They just made the best of what they had. I had five brothers and one sister. I was next to the youngest.

They had grade schools up there. When I first started school they had just one small school. In fact, I think it was an old home made over into a school. But it was there, and in about a year they built a new school in that same area. Pretty large school, accommodated everybody. Yeah, they were able to go to school and get an education. That is, in grade school, up until eighth grade. As I recall jobs were plentiful. They really didn't help him in getting them. It did happen. One friend would talk to the boss, and the boss would say, "Well, send him in, I have a room for him." Most of the time they were able to get work because even all the young fellows that went away to school and all, they all worked around the mines when they were kids, making a few extra dollars. Of course, in our family they went to work early, because they needed the money. Wages were turned over to the parents. We never kept the money. The father and the mother, they controlled the finances. They'd give us a dollar or two. Later on it got to maybe five dollars. My brother Teofil worked around the mines; he didn't do much of anything else. He got in politics later and in 1926 he was a councilman in Nanticoke, but he was also a very active union worker, and they had no unions at that time to amount to anything. It was hard to get organized. They'd call meetings in one little room somewhere in the hall, and the coal companies would send in stooges and break them up. They had a hard time getting organized in the beginning. They couldn't get it organized. He died many years ago. But he was active. And you know, he was so active that the coal companies didn't like what he was doing and he was blackballed. He couldn't get a job. Before he became councilman. He had to go away to New York to get a job out there in Brooklyn or somewhere, or Newark. He was married. He had a wife. She didn't go on with him, and with all this trouble. My brother Martin worked in the breaker, and I don't think he ever worked inside the mines. Number five colliery. Number five and Number seven were both right here in Nanticoke. But Martin only stayed there for—well, I guess until they went into service. No, even before that. He switched and got into carpentry. He learned to be a good carpenter. That's right, that was before the first World War. And then when the war broke out, they registered, and since Martin was a carpenter, they send him into the shipyards. They figured that they needed the shipbuilders as much as they needed the soldiers, because between Germany and the U.S.A. they needed a lot of transportation. So he landed in the shipyards in Philadelphia and then he transferred from there to Baltimore. He told me he did want to join the army. He went in to get in the service, but they wouldn't take him. They said, "No, we want you where you are needed." So he worked there. And not only that, when he came back out of the service, he came back here and then he went into construction himself. His own construction business, yeah. And he stayed with that. He finished his days with it practically. My third brother Joseph. But Joseph, he died young. He worked around the collieries, and he, too, got in the carpentering end of it, and he also was called during the war into the shipyards in Philadelphia. He stayed in Philadelphia when the war was over, and he came back here. But then he went in business. First of all he had a battery shop on Main Street, where he bought and sold batteries and repaired that. It was a big business in those days. Batteries didn't hold up as long, and they replaced the plates and all, and made a new battery out of an old one.

88

And then he left that and went into the garage and automobile business. He had an agency that sold automobiles for a while and repaired cars. Then from there the family bought this property here in 1920. He came here and started a real trucks and repair service also, and the gas station, they put pumps in. In fact, I always say it was the first drive-in station in Nanticoke. Before that they had curb pumps, but this was a novelty. You drive in off the road and fill up your tank. Of course the old pumps were hand pumps, they weren't operated by twisting your hand. There was even carpentry work around the mines to do. I don't know if they pick up so many skills, but even inside the mine they had to put doors in and "braddish" off certain areas and lock them off. But there were doors everywhere to control that air in there.

Q: What about the timbers and things like that?

ZNANIECKI: Timbers, yeah. They all had loads of timber and the timber was used for propping up all the mines to try to hold the coal up there. I'll never forget when I went in there—this was already later of course—and the miner would fire a shot. There was a lot of smoke and everything else, and then he'd go back into his place and he took his pick—he'd start hitting the ceiling of one. I would run, you know what I mean? But then later on I knew what he was doing. He was knocking down anything that was loose so that it wouldn't come in there and come down on his head. But it was a thrill, just to see that guy go in there. Sure, that's the only way they got the coal. They had to keep firing shots all the time. They drilled what's called the face and then they had a curtain right behind it, so that when the shots were fired they tried to keep as much of that smoke away from themselves as possible until the air goes through, pulls it out there, so they'd go back in and work. Yeah, that was all bombing, that was all firing away. They'd drill big holes and put the dynamite in there and set it off. Bang, another pile of coal would come out, and they'd load that into their cars. They'd build their tracks all the way into the place and the car was there, they'd load it. I'll never forget when I was down there. When you worked they'd tell you, "If you can load a car cold while you're down there, we'll pay you extra money for it." Well, one night I and the motorman decided we're going to load this one car of coal and make ourselves a few extra dollars. This was the first and last car. You didn't realize how big that car was until you started to shovel. Oh my God, we shoveled and we shoveled and we shoveled. We finally got it filled up. We never tried another one. Then we could appreciate how these miners worked. Boy, their shovels were this big, and I'm telling you, they just got in there and loaded that car in no time. They had to be giants.

Testing mine roof, 1920

Miners in cage wait to be lowered, 1919.

Well, my brother Joe died. He got sick in that year, 1927. He died. They called it tuberculosis or pneumonia. They were careless in a way. He worked around the cars and in those days when the gas lines were full, they'd take them off and blow it out, things of that sort. I guess they inhaled a lot of that stuff, and it ruined his lungs. Then there was my brother Stanley. Stanley worked around the mines. I don't think Stanley was ever in the mines. No, he too got into the carpentering end of it first of all, and he worked at that for several years. Stanley was very good at it. He wasn't afraid of heights, he liked to climb anywhere and do anything and he wasn't afraid of it. I guess the bosses at that time thought that he had something that they could use, so they made him a shaft engineer on the—you know what the coal shaft is, where they bring the coal up and down, and the people. It's a steam-drive thing. You had to have a lot of guts and a lot of self control to run those things, because if you made a mistake they go through or drop somebody down and kill them. And they had to be fast. They insisted on so many cars coming up that shaft a day, and you had to do it, so you were just there all day. Needed a guy who was pretty stable, and Stanley was. I know when I started to work, he was on that shaft and I went down there. He gave me a ride down. Well, he did it purposely, of course. I'm telling you, that shaft went down so fast you thought you were falling down. You weren't riding down, you were just falling down into the mines. If they had men on there, they didn't have any coal. But after they got the men down, then all day long they were bringing coal up and down.

Q: Where were your parents? Did they stay in the Honeypot area?

ZNANIECKI: No, we stayed there until 1916. They were just building the school there, that's how I remember it. The school was 1915, but by the time they finished it was 1916. They bought a lot right up the street here on Loomis Street and by that time Martin and Joe and Teofil, they were already pretty handy as carpenters and they had a lot of friends and neighbors. This is amazing. They bought this lot and they built that home, between the parents and the children and some of their friends. They'd have a keg of beer every once in a while and a little bit of food— they built that home and built a beautiful home. Cost nothing but the material costs. For two thousand dollars. That was there and it looks good today as the day they put it up.

In 1922 Joseph was in business already up there, and he liked this area. This was a stocking mill here. Ambrose West had a stocking mill. So he persuaded the parents to buy the place (East Main Street) and together they pitched in and came over here and bought this whole corner. They put it in a lot of money. They put that glass front in, and they put the apartments in. They put some extensions back out and made it a nice building with two apartments and a showroom and a garage. They put the pumps out front and they had a real nice business place. Well, he didn't last long, the poor fellow. Then when Joe died in 1927, I had to take over. I was next in line. That's when I started in business. First of all I quit school. I was delivering parcel post first, when I was going to school, and then I got a job carrying mail. I had a steady job as a mailman, back in the hills. But that didn't appeal to me. I thought, why, what the heck am I going to do, carry this bag up here for the rest of my days? Then I quit. And I left that and I went back to high school. I quit high school, see, I went back to finish my high school. That's the time I worked in the mines at night, and went to school up here. But yes, I delivered parcel post and I carried mail, and of course I clerked a lot. When you were a substitute for a while you substitute as a clerk or a carrier.

Q: But your brothers went into the mines and your father went in. Why didn't you want to go in?

ZNANIECK: But they had no choice. By that time, in my case I saw that there was a better job in the post office. Joe was already working in his garage and in business, and that gave me a little more incentive too, and he had a car that we could use a little bit because he had it. That was why I went into the post office. But they didn't pay much money in those days. The carrier got about eighteen hundred dollars, which was considered one of the good jobs for a young man. Anyway, I couldn't stand the thought of walking back in that hill for the rest of my days at eighteen years old. So I quit and I went back. Then in '27 when Joe died, I wound up in here and I stayed in here. We eventually expanded a little, we had another station down on Broadway with railroad and storage tanks. We got into the gas and oil business in a pretty big way. We had a station back in the hill, and one in Glen Lyon, one in Ashley—we had about five stations going. Just the brother and I. Originally the parents owned it, owned his property, and of course, by that time Dad wasn't working, so we took care of them. It worked both ways. We had the use of the property, and we took care of them also. They never wanted for anything because we started to do pretty well. Dad used to help out even in the mornings before we got up. He'd probably be out there six in the morning to open the station and sell gas. He was already retired then. That's right, yeah. They lived right here, and we supported them. They were helpful, but we really supported them for all their good, and make enough money to keep them and ourselves. Yeah, it was all right. It worked out fine. We expanded a little. There were tough times. There were times when you didn't known when your next piece of bread—even in business. Sometimes it got a little tough. But altogether when I started, that time between the first World War and the second World War, they were the good days in this area. They were really booming. Everybody had money. As I said, even when I went to school and worked in the mines, you'd load an extra car and you got a few extra dollars for it. The miners would load it and wait and they'd work a couple extra hours and get an extra shift—it was really a boom town. That's when the population went up to twenty-eight, pretty close to thirty thousand people here in Nanticoke. But it was the mines that did it. Everybody worked in the mines and they were making money, making a lot of money, good money. They built homes until the Crash came, 1929, and this area didn't suffer until two or three years after that. The coal mines closed down slowly. We didn't feel that crunch as fast as the factories and all, because they shut down. We kept moving until about 1933. And then the Depression really started. Oil came in, and oil was cheap, and oil was cleaner. To the older people, oil was easier to handle. It really took the coal market away. In my case I always consider myself pretty lucky, because even though the people didn't have a lot of money, they already started to get cars in the early thirties, and they had gasoline cheap—fifty cents you get three gallon, for a dollar you get seven gallon. But they were driving. Then of course the service along with it, little repairs, lubrication, tires, and all that put together. We did very well, we had a nice business going. So all through that Depression I wasn't really hurting.

Q: Don't you become police chief eventually?

ZNANIECKI: I did in 1934 and '35. Well, in business I had a friend, Harry Farrow. He was a friend of John Fine, who was the political leader. And Harry come in for gas, and he said, "Vince, you've got a little time. There's a police chief job open now. Why don't you take it?" And I thought, "What have I got to lose? I'm not on a shift here." By this time we had people working for us and all. So I took it, in '34-'35. And then in '35 my friends decided—well, I think you ought to run for office. I was pretty popular. I mean the business. We did some advertising, you know, and the name was well known. So I did. I ran for office, and I ran on a Republican ticket. I think my father would disown me, because they were all Democrats. I figured that's the only place I never got any assistance from them. Anyway, I ran, and believe it or not the whole ticket lost. I was the only one that won, and by just a few votes. In fact, they were sitting down in the room and discussing this thing, and it looked bad, and I started home. I thought, "Well, I tried." Pretty soon, somebody yelled back, "Hey Vince, come on back, it looks like you may win." City councilman. The town was changed to a city and there was four councilmen and a mayor. So I won by forty or fifty votes is all. Nevertheless, I won, and I was councilman.

Q: Was John Fine Mr. Republican at that time?

ZNANIECKI: Yes he was. Well, he was just one. I think he had some fellows around him, I know, that were probably shrewder politically than even John Fine. He was judge later, but before that he was just an attorney, and he had some State jobs, and then he'd drifted into politics with a fellow by the name of Dave Vaughn from Nanticoke. Dave was a school director. Man, you never saw such an organization. They had a fellow by the name of Ray Livingstone, an attorney. He was their soliciter in Nanticoke. I would say that he and Dave Vaughn worked with Fine. When the organization got tough, you know, they had loads of money. They were loaded with money. In those days, everything was open—slot machines were going, crap joints were open, even were functioning. But all these fellows were kicking in.

Q: They were kicking into the political machine so that the government wouldn't close them down, is that what you are saying?

ZNANIECK: Right, right. That's it exactly. And for a while nobody cared. It was just wide open and it was going. But these fellows were making thousands and thousands of dollars. I know Cap Williams was the boss down here, and Dave Vaughn. Dave Vaughn finally went into the county setup and Cap controlled Nanticoke. We were pretty friendly, even though later on I switched to a Democrat, but we always remained friends, even with Fine. Cap told me many times, he said, "Vince, we collect fifteen, twenty thousand dollars down here for a campaign, and spend maybe five, six or seven." So they had that much left over. That's how much money just was flying in all these gambling joints and all. They were making contributions head over heels. They were loaded with money.

That union fight between Maloney and the regular United Mine Workers was during my time as chief. That was in 1935—'34 and '35 I think it started. We had to ask for State police. We have about fifteen, twenty State police living right in Nanticoke, sleeping there in apartments. Yeah, the State rented them, and they of course reinforced. We have about sixteen men, but we couldn't patrol at all, because it wasn't like a fight between the union and the company, it was a fight between two unions. So the one union wanted to go to work, and we had to protect them going to work because that was the law. They weren't on strike. They weren't fighting the company or anything, they were fighting themselves. So it was our job to protect them going to work. And at the same time these independents were out there fighting and throwing stones and everything else, and trying to stop these people from going to work. It was a fight amongst two unions, and it was bitter at times. I always tell the story about I'm leaving here and I put my uniform on because they wouldn't let me out the door otherwise. And believe it or not, they respect the uniform to a certain extent. I'll never forget. I went down this road here and right to the next street and when the car's making a turn there's a woman out there, believe it or not with a big rock. She took this rock and banged it right into the windshield and broke it. Not mine, no, one of the workers'. And there I am, right there, right behind it. I had to stop, of course, and help the guy but I got hold of the woman. We couldn't arrest them or take them to jail, we had no place to put them. There was no room. No, they weren't fit for a woman in there. So I didn't bother. I had my club and I got hold of the woman and I give her a whack over the backside and I said, "Get out of here and stay out of here. This is no place for you. This is wrong. Now go on home." Well, she did. Many of those things happened.

Q: Did women become involved in labor protests?

ZNANIECKI: Only in these times when there was fighting. There was a fight between the two unions and of course it caused a lot of unrest between the people in the area, those that wanted to go to work and [those that] didn't, and it reached into the family. It was a bad situation. I know of another incident where just two of us policemen down on West Main Street—there must have been three thousand miners from the one side and two or three or four thousand from the other side, and we stood right in between them. Luckily, they had enough respect for the policemen not to start a riot. Slowly by talking and persuading them we broke that up. While I'm standing there I see there's a big coal bank, and somebody knocked one man off of that bank, I guess maybe about seventy-five feet or so, and rolled him down. Then the guys on the bottom over there started to heel him, and, of course, I'm the chief of police with a gun in my pocket. I'll never forget this. I had to run over there and pull my gun for the first time in my life. They respected it. They walked away. I said, "I'm sorry, I'm responsible for this man's life. I can't let you do this." So they broke away and we loaded them in. They would have killed him, I think. I really do, yeah. Nobody was killed, but I think in that one incident they probably would have. I don't know, they just didn't like the guy or something. But it was a bitter fight.

The abuses in the mines were terrible. Mine bosses—they [the miners] had no protection, no union—they could do as they pleased. They [UMW] didn't do enough for those people. They were interested in organizing and collecting the money and looking to a stronger union, I imagine, eventually. I don't think they did that deliberately, but I guess they weren't strong enough to help these people at that time. The people got tired of waiting and along comes Maloney and promises all these things. They were ripped off, they were being cheated. They're paid by the yard, maybe even make five yards. They'd pay them for three or four. And they'd load so many cars and they'd knock off these cars. The bosses, everyone would do that.

Q: Was this widespread?

ZNANIECKI: Yes. Yes it was. My father used to tell me about how they were cheated on the work that they did. They did a lot of work and they were never paid the full amount. There's where all the grievances came from. They were hurt. And there were favorites. They'd give the fellows that—you know, there were even rumors that some of them were kicking back to the bosses because they had finer places where the coal was better, easier to mine, could load more cars and make much money. All these things—the miners were bitter, because they were working hard and working like mules and they weren't paid even what they should have been paid legally, by what the company was offering and the mine bosses were depriving. That was the cause of the unrest between the two unions. They just didn't figure that John L. Lewis and the regular union was doing enough for them, so naturally they were reaching out for anybody that was trying to give them a hand. Eventually the Anthracite fell apart; Maloney was killed. I don't know what year John L. Lewis got the checkoff. That was the beginning of the strong United Mine Workers Union. That made them. Every payday they didn't have to go along and sit at the desk in the union hall and collect this money. It came directly to them, right from the coal company. That was the beginning of John L. Lewis' United Mine Workers.

We just kept them apart, that's all. We never let anybody congregate or get together so that there could be any real violence, besides throwing stones occasionally. It never developed into where anybody was killed or hurt or anything. We had just enough police protection just to keep them apart. Those that wanted to go to work, we followed them around and let them go. At first, the others couldn't do it out in the open because we were there to protect them.

Q: Speaking of churches, did any of the priest or clergy become involved in any of the union activity or the political activity? Would they speak out? For example, would you go to church on a Sunday, would it be likely that you would hear the priest talk about the unions?

ZNANIECKI: No. I think the priests stayed out of it. They did not go into that at all. No, they took no part in it. Of course between the two miners [unions] they couldn't. Their parishioners were—some belonged to this, some belonged to that. But even before that I don't remember priests being active in it at all. They were mostly interested in religion, and I think at that time—as today, they still don't want the Catholic priests to be too active in politics. And they didn't then either. Father Dreier, he was in Plymouth. But he took the other course. He became a stockholder in the Glen Alden Coal Company, and that way he did a lot of favors for his parishioners. He got a lot of the men as fire bosses and other bosses. Through his influence he got a lot of work for them.

The fire boss was the fellow that went in early in the morning, long before the miners went to work, and he had a gas line. He'd check these spots to see if there was not too much gas in there, so that they could go in there safely and work. So he had to do that every morning. If he started, say four or five in the morning, and then put in his eight hours, finally—but he'd finish his eight hours from four or five on and then he'd go home. But they checked those places so there wasn't too much gas. If there was, the miners also had lamps and they checked it, but you could be careless or a spark fly if there's too much gas. It was a prized job and it paid more. Fire boss was considered one of the better jobs. The other priest that was, I think, active in politics was Father Lemondusky. He was a great friend of John Fine. He was at the St. Mary's Church in Nanticoke. But there again, he wasn't active in preaching politics but he became a very good friend of John Fine and he, too, did many favors for his parishioners. He got them jobs and favors and things of that sort, he played that angle up. He and John Fine were very friendly. But as for taking an active part in politics, trying to elect or defeat somebody, no, they didn't do that.

We had no bootlegging of coal in this area. The coal companies controlled every foot of it. Every foot of it. They owned, controlled it and they were in charge. They told you how much tax they were going to pay, and how much they weren't going to pay. They controlled it. I'll tell you of another incident when I was on council. I started to yell a little bit about [coal companies] not paying enough taxes. . . And believe it or not, I had a friend visit me, and by that time Stanley was already shafting—that was in '36 and '37—and this fellow told me, he said, "Your brother has a nice job, Vin. If you want him to keep it. . ." And that puts you in an awful spot. And I thought, well, I don't have so much to gain; I'm not going to save the world by increasing the tax a little, so I had to soft-peddle it. I felt sorry for Stanley. Ye gods, I wouldn't want him to lose that job. He'd probably never get another one if they blackballed him entirely. But we got along. I finally got to be friendly with them and we did the best we could. They controlled it. They were in the driver's seat and they had their taxpayer's organization. Fortunately, they didn't ask us to do anything that was wrong. Their biggest interest was in holding down taxes, that was all. That's all you want, and honesty, because that keeps taxes down. So we did. We had in our administration—it was good government. They [coal companies] controlled every foot of this valley. In fact, when I was on the council and in business, I wanted to buy a lot on the other end of town on what they call the Middle Road and Prospect Street. There I already knew these people. Glen Alden, that's who owned it, and we were in their office, and the mayor, Mayor Williams, went up with me and a couple of the other councilmen. We sat down and discussed it, and I said, "I'd like to buy that piece of ground out there. I'm in the gas business, and it would be a good spot." So he thought it over and he said, "I'm sorry, Vince. If I sell you that, you'll build a station, you'll light it up, and the first thing you know they'll want more money for the land all around it." So they turned me down. Later on we had a chamber of commerce here, and I was on that. We had many interested, many industries that we got interested in coming here. Well, they thought it was a good labor market. There was nothing else here and they thought it was fine to come in here—plenty of people, and they were hard workers, willing to work and wanting to work and hard workers. They thought it was a good, nice area. But the minute they start inquiring, they got to the Chamber of Commerce, and they wouldn't come back to us. It was the end. As true as I sit here, they wouldn't come in, they couldn't come in. They knew they couldn't get the land from the coal company.

Into the forties when the children were graduating from schools, they had no work. They had to go look somewhere else. Many of the people who weren't too old, even they left. But that was already the later '30's and early '40's. They started to drift away from here. They went to New Jersey, New York, Connecticut, Maryland. Mostly they followed relatives and friends. Some of them went anywhere. They heard that there was work there, and most of them got jobs. There was still work in some of those areas. I think the coal miner had a reputation of being a hard worker, and they wanted to hire them. And he was. So, most of them—but mostly through friends that they knew, they say, "Why, I'm in Maryland, I think you can get a job down here." Or New Jersey, or New York, or Connecticut. That's where I think most of them went. They didn't go much beyond that. Some of them went as far as Michigan because they had friends out there, but those are the only states that I know of that a lot of them went. And of course the young people, they all had to go. They just couldn't get work around.

Q: What about your father—did he ever talk much about what he wanted for you? Did he ever consciously come out and say I want you to go in the mines or not go in the mines, or did he leave it up to you?

ZNANIECKI: He never wanted us to go in the mines if we could help it. I guess that's how Joe got into business. He figured that the best place for us would be to get into some kind of business, and he encouraged it very much. That's how I think Joe got into it, because Dad wanted him to do it. He didn't want us in the mines, no. That was the last thing he wanted. So that's how we got in business.

I forgot, but they bought things they could get kickbacks on. There was enough in the pavings, but they bought all these things they could get kickbacks on. And they got caught at it. We had a bad government for a while, very bad. They was taken to court there on that particular case, but Fine was the judge and they squashed it somehow. Young attorney that represented the taxpayers, he wasn't too smart, and they killed it. That was in my early days. When I got in there in 1960, we already changed. They had some good men in there. The coal company's Taxpayers Association used to come down to us and commend us on what we were doing. They said, "We don't know how you're operating. Why don't you raise the millage or something and get yourself more money?" I said, "Who's going to pay?" And the other councilmen felt the same way. Why, these people are on relief, they're getting one hundred, one hundred fifty dollars; we can't raise the taxes. But they used that and they went around and they showed others how a city can really operate if they have to. I was proud of it. I really was. It was tied in with the decline of the coal companies. The coal companies didn't care how much you stole, if you didn't raise the taxes. So what they did instead of raising taxes, they floated bond issues. It was going in debt. Every time they needed more money, what they paid off, they'd float some more bonds. Right, coal companies didn't care. Of course, they couldn't go too far. But they didn't raise the millage, they just kept paying off these bonds and just postponing the thing.

With all due respect to the coal companies and their Taxpayers Association, they didn't condone stealing. They didn't exactly go in there and prosecute them, but they didn't advocate it, no one did. It was just a matter of time that taxes would go up. So in the meantime whatever they could rake off in these things, these fellows did, and between what they collected and what they raked off, they made themselves some nice extra money. This started to change when the Fine organization broke up. The government's more autonomous, they were on their own more or less, they didn't get any pressure from the county. Luckily, we got some good men in finally. They didn't have as much money to play with because there was no coal company taxes by that time, and they had to collect it all from the people. So in the latter '30's, already, this thing started to change. They were free, and we got some good men; they were operating and Nanticoke finally got into really good government.

I'll never forget when I was mayor, we started on this housing; you had to go down to Harrisburg and get approval from Public Affairs or one of those departments. We got into a room and whoever was there run in and said, "The Nanticoke officials are here. They want to talk about housing, and they have an appointment." "Oh send them in, send them in." You know, welcome with open arms, because we had a good record, we had a good reputation, and that's another reason why they got so much housing and redevelopment. We were the first. We took advantage of everything because by this time this government was good. They were operating and they had a good credit rating, so we took advantage of everything. Redevelopment, housing, streets—we got streets paved at half price. One year we paved around twenty or thirty streets, all over the place, and only paid half because the government paid the other half. Only because we had a good operating government and a good credit rating. So that worked out fine, and until this day I think that Nanticoke city—I couldn't say the same for the school board—they kept on, I don't say that from experience, but from what we knew they were in the same organization. . .and we worked hard on them, tried to tell him, "Look boys, the best government and the best way to get re-elected is to have a good government. If you can go out and tell the taxpayers you're doing a good job, you'll get re-elected." But how can you stop the stealing if the money is available? Many times I would defend them to such an extent. I would say, "Well, all right, you're sitting in this council and along comes a contractor and he says, 'Well, here's five thousand dollars for you boys, or here's ten thousand dollars, boys.' You have no obligations. You take it." But there was obligations. They could do as they pleased, they could do slipshod work. I know, we were offered it once when I was down there. It was a paving contractor. We turned it down. Actually, we turned it down, because we didn't want to be obligated. Anyway it was two, three, four, five hundred. It was ridiculous.